Russia, Freaks and Foreigners
Three Performance Texts

Russia, Freaks and Foreigners
Three Performance Texts

James MacDonald

intellect Bristol, UK / Chicago, USA

To Mother, Pop, Susan and Inna
Four of God's truly elect

First Published in the UK in 2008 by
Intellect Books, The Mill, Parnall Road, Fishponds, Bristol, BS16 3JG, UK

First published in the USA in 2008 by
Intellect Books, The University of Chicago Press, 1427 E. 60th Street, Chicago,
IL 60637, USA

A catalogue record for this book is available from the British Library.

Cover Design: Gabriel Solomons
Copy Editor: Holly Spradling
Typesetting: Mac Style, Nafferton, E. Yorkshire

ISBN 978-1-84150-186-4

Printed and bound by the Charlesworth Group, Wakefield.

CONTENTS

INTRODUCTION

Russia, Freaks and Foreigners: Three Performance Texts does not constitute a trilogy in the formal sense, but several things serve to unite the texts and to justify their collection as a unified book. They are all texts whose first performances were directed by one man. Two of the three were written as part of an undergraduate module in interpretive acting, led by the same man. All three share thematic concerns with various forms of difference. Consummately, I hope, they provide the theatre reader with a dynamic experience of this complex and far-reaching subject – personally, socially, culturally.

Performance texts are primarily for performance, and their dissemination in book form necessitates a discussion of their performance characteristics. This is especially true of new texts (whose performance history is extremely short). I have been ideally served in this respect by having accompanying essays by colleagues of long standing who can discuss the texts in ways that newly published texts are not often discussed in print. Martin Harvey, who directed the performances, discusses the theatrical qualities of the texts; Peter Thomson has known my work for thirty years and gives a historical perspective on its genesis; Thomas Fahy has done extensive work on the literary/dramatic nature of difference and brings this to bear in a detailed analysis of *Bread and Circus Freaks*; Su Elliott closes the volume with her reflections on what it was like to perform one of these texts. Their views were expressed independently, and it may well be that they even contradict one another in certain respects. But this is the essence of critical discourse, and any author is privileged indeed to have his/her work focused in this way. Whatever they say, each contributor is a MacDonald expert as well as a distinguished practitioner, and their comments can only enhance the reader's isolated perusal of these texts.

As for my own view (for what it is worth), I have always sought to employ disability much as Dostoyevsky uses epilepsy, to comment on the human condition as a whole. Many writers have used deformity in this way (Rabelais, Gogol, Nathanael West, Carson McCullers), and I feel in kindred spirit with them. *Bread and Circus Freaks*, for example, was intended to be a contemporary re-working of the Russian vaudeville, a comic play often centred on mistaken identity. As Peter Thomson has noted, questions of identity have rarely been absent from all my work, and Martin Harvey has given a partial glimpse into the reasons why. Transforming life into artefact, with regard to *Circus Freaks*, I meant the title to refer to all the characters, as Thomas Fahy notes, and for each character to do a 'turn' in presenting her/his take on society. Each is somehow an outsider, and each has something distinctive to say about society. Without their separateness, they would not be outsiders.

I meant the play to be funny, and audiences have definite views not only on the subjects they accept as comic but also on the ways this comedy can be purveyed. Peter Thomson talks about this in relation to a 1984 play he helped produce in London. Peter is quite right that the agent who was helping me at the time had serious commercial misgivings about disability as a subject. She said she had had a terrible time trying to market *A Day in the Death of Joe Egg* and that the characters in my play were even more depressing to watch. A *Times* reviewer seemed to bear this out when he averred that *Whose Life Is It Anyway?* offers a far better view of disability than my play. But inasmuch as Brian Clarke's play is really about euthanasia, its disability statement could almost be seen as fascistic. And I ear-wigged on two patrons in wheelchairs who said of my play's verisimilitude, 'He'd have to be disabled (in order) to know that.'

Perhaps Peter is correct when he suggests that it takes direct knowledge of what he calls 'the other side' to fully appreciate depictions of it. But shying away from a subject (for whatever reason) is hardly the best way to respond to it, and theatre has always been in the vanguard when it comes to tackling difficult subjects. Tom Fahy has done splendid work in examining the whole history of the freak show. But outlawing such exhibitions may simply result in removing 'deformity' from the social agenda. One aim of the publication of all three texts is to place issues of deformity and dislocation squarely before the public in such a way that they must respond beyond polite detachment, and unrestrained laughter is a clear sign of honest engagement. In this way the performance of all three texts was an attempt to push back two boundaries – presenting the subject at all, and then challenging audiences to find the displays comic. Neither aim was carried out in a spirit of hostility toward the audience. I was not asking anyone to confront suppressed prejudices. But equally, failure to acknowledge a subject can be as cruel as actively promulgating it. For all the brutality of some of the characters' behaviour, they do not flinch from the subjects of deformity and dislocation, and their candour was what we attempted to bring before audiences.

This was certainly so in the case of Martin Harvey's production of *Bread and Circus Freaks*, and so it has remained in our work with students on the other two texts in this volume, all of which has summoned a tremendous amount of courageous commitment from the performers. This may even exceed one author's fondest dream(s). Performers in the first play were willing to risk unpopularity on the progressive fringe to achieve something of devastating novelty, and then student performers have been eager to commit themselves to work that goes beyond progressive curriculum, involving workshop engagement with issues that have remained hidden for far too long. I cannot exaggerate the extent of this courage; indeed, I have no wish to in paying the fullest tribute to all the contributors to this volume (among whom I am happy to include Sam King, Roberta Mock and everyone else at Intellect). What you have done here is genuinely remarkable, as the life of this volume will clearly bear out. For this reason alone, I have high hopes (and unstinting gratitude) for it.

James MacDonald

PART ONE: TEXTS

BREAD AND CIRCUS FREAKS

A One Act Vaudeville

First performed at the Finborough Theatre, London, on 6 March 2002, under the direction of Martin Harvey and with the following cast:

PANIA ANDREYEVNA	Su Elliott
INNA IGOROVNA	Leah Fells
MARIANNA SELIGMAN	Leslie O'Hara
OSIP PISHCHIK	Michael Bottle
VOLKOV	Stephen Harvey

Design	Kamal Desei
Russia Consultant	Inna Rodina

In the countryside surrounding Petersburg, winter.

Marianna (Leslie O'Hara) and Pania (Su Elliott) struggle for control of Inna (Leah Fells). *Bread and Circus Freaks*, Finborough Theatre, March 2002. Photo: Marilyn Kingwill.

Settlement No. 7, some 70 kilometres from Petersburg, a village impacted by snow and by circumstance – the remnants of a collective farm. A bread shop immediately after the morning delivery. PANIA ANDREYEVNA, 42 but looking 15 years older and very thin, supports INNA IGOROVNA through the back door. INNA is nearly twenty but looks five years younger. Most distinctively, though, she is heavily spastic from cerebral palsy. PANIA stations INNA on a chair and begins lifting the bread trays from the floor to the counter.

INNA (*After watching her for several seconds.*): I wish I could help you.

PANIA: You what? (*Preoccupied.*) No...you can't do it.

INNA: If we could maybe carry the trays –

PANIA: ...I know. We'd feel like millionaires. I'd feel like a millionaire anyway. I'd feel like I didn't need to work...and then I wouldn't employ you...and then you wouldn't work...You'd be an outcast, for people to take pity on or worse...because pity soon turns to contempt...and then you might starve...they'd look for your footprints in the snow...and then maybe some night – or maybe first light – someone would discover the corpse of an under-fed girl...half-eaten by wolves...and then they'd say, 'Wasn't that the waif that used to work for Pania Andreyevna? I'm sure of it.' And then they'd come looking for me...and charge me with murder after the fact...and all because I let you help me lift the trays. I wouldn't feel much like a millionaire then, would I? A million's not much good against a murder rap, is it? Especially if it's all an illusion. You can't pay a murder judge with it. 'If she felt she had a million, she could have showed more compassion to poor Inna Igorovna.' That's what they'd say...that's the verdict they'd bring in on me. It's worth a little inconvenience to be spared a fate like that, now wouldn't you say?

She's been working the while.

INNA: I wish I could help you.

PANIA: Oh-ho, you're helping me. You think I'm running a charity ward? You're serving our hungry horde while I put my feet up in back. Maybe I'll even fall into the third degree of sleep...so that when you have a riot here – when demand far exceeds our supply – you won't be able to wake me. I won't know anything about it. What do you reckon to that? I'm throwing you in at the deep end, my Inka. I don't believe in charity.

INNA: We don't have wolves here, do we?

PANIA: I didn't say I was throwing you to the wolves – I said –

INNA: ...half-eaten by wolves...if you let me go. Don't you remember? Were you just trying to scare me?

PANIA: I was trying to show you the nonsense you're talking – you could help me lift the trays. I can't do it – I don't see how on earth you think you can. (Calculating.) One, two, three...eight, nine...nine. There isn't going to be enough brown. I told them last time to make it four dozen. They can't hear straight – they've given me four dozen white. Deaf bastards! Well, I thought I was doing you a favour, my darling, but now it looks like –

INNA: You've done me lots of favours, Pania Andreyevna. You've given me this job, for a start...

PANIA: I mean I put up a notice the delivery was going to be late...just to give us time to ourselves.

INNA: Do people really read notices? I don't think so.

PANIA: ...well, with four dozen white loaves, and next-to-no brown...you'd better believe they'll do something constructive. Otherwise, they'll be taking our blood before midday.

INNA: You're not serious.

PANIA: How long have I been selling bread? You'd better believe they'll be asking for bread... and then taking our blood just as soon as we've run out. (A beat.) Can you use a hunter?

INNA: What's a hunter?

PANIA: ...or maybe it'd be all right if you just point.

INNA: I'm sure I can point, but what's – ?

PANIA: A hunting rifle, of course, are you that naive?

INNA: You mean you...fire on people?

PANIA: Yeah, well, mainly I just point.

INNA: And does it work?

PANIA: If it didn't, I'd be shooting at them, wouldn't I? It works, all right. People round here are such cowards.

INNA: So they wouldn't really take our blood. You were just pretend–

PANIA: What are you talking about? They'd certainly try if the delivery was like it was today, and if I didn't have my hunter.

INNA: My God...

PANIA *(Overlapping.)*: What do you think I got it for – effect? They'll try it with you – you'll see.

INNA: I don't want to fire on people!

PANIA: I'd better stay awake then.

INNA: You never told me it was going to be dangerous.

PANIA: What'd you think they were, friends? Furry bunny rabbits?

INNA: All right, I admit, I thought one or two thieves, maybe.

PANIA: Oh, you did, did you? There wouldn't be thieves round here, darling. We've grown up together, you know? We're just crazy, that's all. Especially when we're forced to eat white when they haven't brought brown. Then we're apt to grow a little irate, you know? And then the only thing that can calm us is a hunter, even if it's only pointed at us.

INNA: My mother heard...I guess she saw it on television...The President made a big speech.

PANIA: It couldn't have been on television.

INNA: Oh, you know the one I mean?

PANIA: One what?

INNA: ...speech – the one he just made.

PANIA: It wouldn't have made any difference, if he made it on television. Your mother couldn't have seen it.

INNA: What makes you so sure?

PANIA: ...we only have radio here...and the radio said the television tower burnt down.

INNA: I don't think you –

PANIA: Are you simple as well as naive? I'm telling you straight – the whole place is in cinders. That's what the radio said.

INNA: Well, yes, I know that...

PANIA: Well, then, what are you – ?

INNA: ...but only one tower. Not enough to stop broadcasting.

PANIA: Your mother must have heard it on the radio, like everybody else.

INNA is vexed.

INNA: Anyway, the President issued the warning that Russia is steadily dying off. What do you say, d'you think it's true?

PANIA: I know it – there's not enough brown.

INNA: He means, she said, because older people are dying off faster than babies are being born.

PANIA: Older people, I tell you, aren't the problem – it's that people producing the babies are dying off. Older people don't produce, do they. They're better dead ... in the ground...as manure.

INNA: But who would you say are the others – soldiers and people like that?

PANIA: Russians aren't getting their fibre... (*Shouting.*) ...when all they'll deliver is mouldy white bread.

INNA: It's not mouldy, is it?

PANIA: It gets mouldy – nobody eats it. (*A beat.*) You like soldiers, do you? You'd like to be raped by a soldier?

INNA: No, you said...I thought soldiers must be who you meant...they'd all died.

PANIA: Not in my lifetime. There's not enough of 'em. In the history books, maybe. Yes, in the history books about wars. Is that your schoolgirl fantasy, is it? Foreign wars with Russian soldiers raping the flesh off you? Sex isn't that good.

INNA: That's not my fantasy, Madame Pania.

PANIA: Ha – says you.

INNA: It must be yours.

PANIA: It's nobody's, that's the whole point.

INNA: That's what the President says.

PANIA: What does the President know that I don't...except where to find some brown bread? About sex, though, he can't tell me nothing. And what is this 'Madame Pania'? We've established I'm no millionaire.

INNA: But I wanted to show I respect you.

PANIA: Be a good girl then. Don't say 'Madame' just so you can give me an argument. I'd rather you were rude and then listened to some good advice.

INNA: I listen.

PANIA: You can't talk and listen.

INNA: That's called 'discussion'.

PANIA: It's called showing me no respect.

INNA: All right. I'm sorry.

PANIA: So you should be. (A beat.) I don't hold discussions with people. It's just the way I'm made. God said at my birth, 'This one won't discuss anything with anyone. We can make sure she has a pretty face, strong hands. We'll give her other things to get by with in life. But when other people hold their discussions, it'll be like she's not in the room.' So – that's my personal message from God, that's my fate. I'm healthy enough, good and strong.

INNA: You can produce babies.

PANIA: Oh, yes, my insides still work. My mother had me when she was 47. There's only one thing wrong with birth in this village. You discuss things. Do you know what that is? Shall I tell you? The men who are still living are all past it. I'm wasting away.

INNA: ...so the President's right.

There is a thumping against the door.

PANIA: Unless I want to produce with a goat.

INNA: What was that?

PANIA: The billygoat mounting the nanny.

INNA: Oh, you're joking.

INNA crosses the space to get a better look at the goats from one of the two windows. Her walk is asymmetrical and slow.

Somebody should take a photograph – that's hilarious.

PANIA: Maybe you should still be at school.

INNA *(Still amused.)*: Why's that? It's true – they're really making love.

PANIA: You've seen dogs do it.

INNA: Not that often...and somehow it's not so funny.

PANIA: You should maybe study mathematics.

INNA: Why? I know what's what – I'm not that innocent.

PANIA: With mathematics on your mind, the sight of the goats might not be so funny.

INNA: What's wrong with having a laugh?

PANIA: There's no men, just like there's not enough brown. So what's the point of liking sex?

INNA: No, you can't call that sex – it's just funny.

PANIA *(A beat.)*: Maybe you should study biology.

A pause.

INNA *(Trying to peer through the window.)*: Who'd have thought they could do it in this cold?

PANIA: They were forced to push the train for the final kilometre.

INNA: Eh? What was that, Mad – Pania Andreyevna?

PANIA: It doesn't matter in the least. Go on with your dreaming.

INNA *(Turns back to PANIA.)*: No, I'm sorry. What did you say?

PANIA: Don't apologize, Inna. It gets on my nerves.

INNA: But you said something I didn't hear. I want to know what it was. Unless you don't want to tell me. Did God say, 'You mustn't repeat yourself'?

PANIA: Let's leave God up in heaven. I was talking about the bread train.

INNA: What, and there being no brown?

PANIA: Not enough brown, I said.

INNA: Well, other than pointing your hunter –

PANIA: ...and the fact that you take no interest at all. I was only trying to tell you how the bread train had to be pushed the last bit.

INNA: What do you mean, pushed? That's terrible...isn't it?

PANIA: It's bloody hard work.

INNA: What – you mean you did it, too?

PANIA: All the women helped.

INNA: What did the men do, stand and watch?

PANIA: There were no men.

INNA: So who did the driving?

PANIA: What the hell does that matter?

INNA: Well, if it was a man, it matters quite a lot, I'd have thought.

PANIA: Who else would they get to drive the damn train? But where were the others to push it? That's what I'm saying. It took fifteen or twenty of us women.

INNA: Well, yes, it would, fifteen or twenty at least. And I'll bet it took you an age and three quarters.

PANIA: It was on a downward incline.

INNA: Yes, all right, but even so...

PANIA: You see what I'm trying to tell you now.

INNA: ...and I see what the President meant.

PANIA: And he doesn't help us. *(Sighs.)* I'm sure he's a great man...he has a great plan for Russia and all that...

INNA: You can't expect him to help you push the train!

PANIA: Fool. I'm not talking about that.

INNA *(A beat.)*: He once lived in Petersburg, you know.

PANIA: Well, I never met him.

INNA: I didn't say you did.

PANIA: Well, then, why bring it up? He once lived in Peters, so what? He should have helped push?

INNA: Now you're making fun of me.

PANIA: Then you can say I don't understand today's youth...that I must be past it. I'm good only for giving out not enough loaves. Our Lord's grace is no longer in me. All right. Let the hungry go on to the city. I want a good long rest.

INNA: ...and let me look after the shop for you.

PANIA: ...when there aren't any people.

INNA: But there will be. You said so yourself.

PANIA: Yeah, too many for one. They'll come in, see you just about standing there...defenceless... and they'll reckon they can exploit the situation. The pushier ones will take immediate advantage... they'll grab the bread without paying...

INNA: But you said they're not thieves.

PANIA: Today's youth have never seen really desperate people. They think they can cope with anything.

INNA: Where'd you get the idea I ever said that?

PANIA: What makes you think you can cope on your own? You're nothing but a kid, a crippled kid at that...living in fantasy land. That may be all right for kids...

INNA: I wish you'd stop saying that.

PANIA: ...but I have to cope in the real world, where trains have to be pushed and then the bread don't get delivered...

INNA: Those sailors who were drowned weren't living in fantasy land...or the soldiers dying in Chechnya.

PANIA: What are you bringing them up for?

INNA: Aren't they just as much youth of today?

PANIA: All right, but you're not dying in Chechnya, are you. What makes you think you can speak for them? Are you a sailor's widow?

INNA: I was just saying what the President said.

PANIA: ...you said he could help us.

INNA: No. I just thought it was interesting he comes from –

PANIA: He's not there now, so what's 'interesting' about it? He's in Moscow sorting out other things. I wouldn't expect him to help us.

INNA: Nor would I.

PANIA: He's got to try to console the poor mothers, poor man. What can he do? He's not God.

INNA: He says he'll look after the children.

PANIA: All their lives? My father was a disabled war veteran they also promised to 'look after'. A blanket, two towels and the message, 'You're lucky you'll die in bed.' 'Look after.'

INNA: And that was in Soviet times. They're saying it's that much worse now.

PANIA: Who are you quoting now...who's 'they'?

INNA: Newspapers, I guess, I don't –

PANIA: They're blasphemers, whoever they are. I don't want to hear you blaspheme. Your mother specifically asked me, she did: 'Look after my Inna, Pania Andreyevna. Make her useful for something. I have to find work in the city.' She's one of my oldest friends.

INNA: Were you Pioneers together?

PANIA: I never made friends in the Pioneers...bunch of hooligans.

INNA: Who, the Pioneers?

PANIA: Of course. *(A beat.)* You were never a Pioneer, were you?

INNA: They wouldn't let me join.

PANIA: You had a lucky escape, let me tell you.

INNA: I'd have been asked to perform feats of skill, which I couldn't...or go rock climbing.

PANIA: They'd have asked all cadets to burn holes in your hands – your torture as their rite of passage.

INNA: The Pioneers?

PANIA: Believe me. Organized criminals, like everybody. Only smaller. Don't look at me like that – I know.

INNA: You mean they tortured you?

PANIA: How could they torture me? I'm not 'unclean'. I could always look after myself. Nobody picked fights with Pania Andreyevna. I'd have bloodied my knuckles on anyone that tried.

INNA: Were you a bit of a bully?

PANIA: What are you talking about, 'bully'? Crazy, are you?

INNA: No, I'm not saying now.

PANIA: Now or ever...is that what you think? You'd characterize me as a bully, would you?

INNA: No, believe me, I –

PANIA: Perhaps next you'll be telling all your crippled friends, 'Pania Andreyevna stuck pins in me, I swear...she stuck lighted fags up my arse.' The Pioneers would do that. I quit the Pioneers when I was younger than you are...and I don't allow smoking in here.

INNA: I was only joking.

PANIA: I'm splitting my sides. You've a warped sense of I-don't-know-what – it isn't humour. Just like the Pioneers.

INNA: Isn't it dangerous to speak out against them?

PANIA: Can anyone hear me? They can't. They've disbanded, like everything else. It's all for nothing. Sailors go down with their ship; towers get razed to the ground. Fucking Chechens won't die – they seem to come out of the ground.

INNA (*Sighing.*): ...and there's no bread.

PANIA: Not enough of it anyway. (*Crossing to a bread tray and selecting a brown loaf for her.*) Here.

INNA: What? No, I don't want –

PANIA: What, you're not like the rest of us? You live on thin air? Are you a sprite?

INNA: No, of course I eat bread, but I have no objection to the white loaf.

PANIA: Unlike the rest of us. Aren't you human? Look here... (*Showing her.*) It's mouldy. There's gobs of mould here and here.

INNA: Well, then no one should eat it...they shouldn't have sent it.

PANIA: No, that's right – you go and complain. You make your way through the snow and the shit, falling down every third step, and you tell them, 'These loaves are mouldy' – and you know what they'll say?

INNA: All right, it's just my opinion.

PANIA: 'You're mouldy yourself, slut' – that's what they'll say. That's their opinion.

INNA (*Taking the white loaf.*): It's not that bad. Look, I can cut the bits off. (*Inspects.*) I think you must be exaggerating. I don't see any –

PANIA: I think you must be dim-witted or something, not to want brown and then not to see any fault in the white.

INNA: Well, take mine, if you're –

PANIA: I've one of my own. Don't be so noble, your first day of work. That's why I say you're dim-witted. They won't bless you for it – they'll just rob me blind. That's not what I'm paying you for, got it straight?

INNA: I'm not talking of anyone else. I want you to have two – you deserve it.

PANIA: 'Deserve' – I deserve to retire. But I'm saying I can't eat two brown before one of them goes mouldy. I eat for balance, you know. Bread and cabbage. Potatoes. And then eggs. We've got dozens of eggs, but no one will touch them. It's brown bread or nothing at all. They'll turn vicious. If you let me have this, back it goes on the pile.

INNA: But your husband may want it instead.

PANIA: What do you know about husbands? He's already got what he wants – his freedom from me. 'They're taking on men at the ironworks' – and him a tractor mechanic. He hit the trail three months back....Bryansk Region, somewhere like that.

INNA: But I'm sure he'll return, like my mother.

PANIA: And I'm sure you're reading your storybooks. I've changed the locks.

INNA: I'm sorry.

PANIA: You think I ought to be? He'd come back crawling from drink, like a mongrel. I wouldn't give him the barn. If your mother comes back, she'll say I'm not feeding you. *(Holding out a brown loaf.)* So I'm supposed to lie?

INNA: She didn't ask you to look after me.

PANIA: You weren't there at the time.

INNA: But I'm nineteen, nearly twenty years old.

PANIA: Nearly twenty and gormless.

INNA *(Fed up, snatching the brown.)*: Gimme the brown.

PANIA *(Holding onto the loaf.)*: I'll put it under the counter, next to mine. *(As she does so.)* They'll do all they can to get them off us, of course. But I've got the hunter good and ready.

INNA: Well, you said so yourself – they're welcome to mine.

PANIA: Let's give them the muzzle instead. *(As she goes back to shifting the loaves.)* Who's looking after you, my dear?

INNA: I thought you said you are.

PANIA: ...I mean with your mother away. Have you gone back to the home?

INNA: Which home – the institution? I haven't been there since I was twelve. I heard they closed it at last, thank the Lord.

PANIA: ...like I said, everything's breaking down.

INNA: I'd call that definite progress. I'm far better off.

PANIA: But the others? They might not have caring mothers with kind employers for friends. What happened to your schoolgirl friends?

INNA: We lost touch.

PANIA: I expect a good many – maybe most – simply died...starved to death. Maybe their carcasses went into animal feed.

INNA: What! Now you're trying to make me feel guilty – I didn't leave them to starve. You talk like –

PANIA: You can be sure it wasn't me.

INNA: It's only your idea they died anyway. Maybe they're –

PANIA: What, only my idea? Another would be that they went into business, emigrated to America, maybe. Yes, that's a definite possibility.

A pause.

INNA: Who was the worst Pioneer you remember?

PANIA: I was.

INNA: No, the meanest...the absolute bully, bordering on sadist. Can you remember?

PANIA: Why do you want to know?

INNA: Every one of the guardians we had was worse. We were simply left there if we so much as soiled our beds or our clothing. I'm talking for days at a time. My memory of a good meal was rice porridge, not even semolina. There was vermin of every description...and the rooms were left untidy and unclean. They'd killed off a lot of my friends through neglect.

PANIA: You're saying you've already been raped.

INNA: That's not exactly what I'm saying.

PANIA: You'll have to tell me 'exactly'.

Somebody tries the door.

INNA: I'm saying it wasn't a home. I remember one time –

PANIA *(Crossing to the window.)*: Oh, my God...more goats.

INNA: Maybe it's our first customer.

INNA crosses to the window, too.

PANIA: We're not ready to open yet. *(Calling.)* Can you hear me all right?

INNA: I told you nobody reads notices. Shall I let them in?

PANIA: You do, and you're going to have to wait on them.

MARIANNA *(From outside.)*: It's cold out here.

PANIA: It's the middle of winter...what does she expect? *(Looking at INNA.)* What's the matter with you?

INNA *(Agitated.)*: I can't possibly wait on her.

PANIA: Ridiculous – why not?

INNA: You do it, please.

PANIA: I told you – it's too early.

INNA: Well, all right, we'll just leave her. *(Whispers.)* It's someone I don't want to see.

PANIA: Oh, for God's sake. *(As INNA starts out the other way.)* Hey, come back here.

INNA: Can't you say I've gone to the toilet or something? Believe me, she won't go away.

PANIA: Yeah, well, we're in business, in case you didn't know it. Are you going to do this with every customer? Fine help I hired. You might as well go home. Don't come back. Stay at home with your Barbie Doll.

INNA *(Part concealed.)*: No, it's just her – I promise.

PANIA: You mean she's a troublemaker? I'll get rid of her then.

They cross – PANIA to the front door, INNA goes somewhere out of sight.

INNA: She's fine...you probably know her, in fact...it's just –

MARIANNA: It's getting colder, if you have any heart...

PANIA: Just give me a fraction of a minute... *(Then to INNA.)* Don't bring your personal problems in here. I don't want you shitting on my doorstep. *(Muttering.)* Her own is too precious, I suppose. *(Calling.)* We don't open till 10 o'clock...like it says on the notice.

MARIANNA *(Still her voice.)*: But it's perishing out here.

PANIA: The notice...you know?

Gesturing to no avail, PANIA now admits MARIANNA SELIGMAN, same age and figure as PANIA but dressed somewhat garishly in a brightly coloured dress and coat and headscarf. Her appearance suggests a gypsy fortune teller. She still tries to get in the door.

MARIANNA: It's bread day – I knew I had to come early.

PANIA: Too early – two hours to go.

MARIANNA: You're usually open by this time.

PANIA: Stock-taking; not for the public.

MARIANNA: But I saw the train come...saw them unloading.

PANIA: There's still the notice...and you could try other places.

MARIANNA: But there are none...you know that.

PANIA: You can't hang that one on me. It's my shop – I suppose I can open when I like. I could even close down the business.

MARIANNA: Don't be silly, Pania Andreyevna.

There's a bit of a game between them with the front door.

PANIA: What if I turned my hunter on you?

MARIANNA: You don't want to go against the law.

PANIA: What would you call what you're doing...trying to break in? (Giving up.) Criminal trespass, they call it.

MARIANNA: You wouldn't really shoot me.

PANIA: Don't press your luck. I was thinking mainly of the door anyway. You're dead meat... but I'm left with a door to fix. It's too cold.

MARIANNA: That's just what I said.

PANIA (Territorial.): There's no fire in here. (Hurriedly sitting on the chair.) Nowhere to sit neither.

MARIANNA: That's all right - I only want bread.

PANIA: I'm afraid I can't allow you to stockpile.

MARIANNA: Would you prefer me to wait?

PANIA: That's right - out there.

MARIANNA: Can I help you at all? What if we moved all the trays?

PANIA: What if we left them alone? You're not going to make out you work here...get round me like that.

MARIANNA: I was just thinking it was easier, that's all.

PANIA: I'll tell you what's 'easier'...

MARIANNA: I told you I'd wait...I don't mind standing...you're kind enough to let me –

PANIA: The quicker I serve you, the sooner you'll go. (Giving her a white loaf.) One to a customer.

MARIANNA: You don't mean that's all they delivered!

PANIA: ...and it might be that's all I ordered. R2.38. And don't even think about asking for brown.

MARIANNA: I'm delighted with this. If you haven't got change yet...

PANIA: Don't you worry about me. I've got change. (Fairly snatching her money and going to the cashbox.) R2.38 from R5...

MARIANNA: I may want something else if it's all right.

PANIA: Tell me now, quick. Eggs?

MARIANNA: We have our own.

PANIA: Aren't you the lucky ones. You never asked me to sell any. If you did, I might be able to let you have brown...today even.

MARIANNA: We're in business with someone in the city.

PANIA: You should support local industry.

MARIANNA: Most would tell you the city is local. Fifteen dozen in one week, sometimes 30.

PANIA: You're making it up! I can't clear that much in six months.

MARIANNA: Well, the village isn't big enough, is it?

PANIA: Getting smaller by the day. Why don't you move to the city? (A beat.) Cabbage or beetroot? Don't tell me you grow that.

MARIANNA: All right, I'll have a cabbage. My daughter goes off to the city this week. That's why I want the bread.

PANIA: With some beets, it'll come to a straight R5.

MARIANNA: Splendid – I can make borsht.

PANIA: We've no sour cream.

MARIANNA: That's all right – Zhenka Rodin supplies me.

PANIA: I'd watch that if I was you – Zhenka Rodin's an alcoholic. His cream is probably tainted with bugs. They put rats in the sausage as well. Rodin's too drunk to know what he's doing. Relieves himself where he stands.

MARIANNA: My family was raised on his produce.

PANIA: And you're still standing? Miraculous.

MARIANNA: And what's this you say about sausages? He doesn't sell any, does he?

PANIA: He's not a villain...no, I never said that.

MARIANNA: It wouldn't matter if he was, if his milk is all right.

PANIA: All I ever said was he drinks too much. And you'd never say 'wouldn't matter' if you died from contaminated milk.

MARIANNA: You're not very cheerful this morning.

PANIA: I'm just speaking the truth. Just trying to warn you, my darling. My bread, for example, is always fresh.

MARIANNA: I can see it is.

PANIA: ...won't have any trouble digesting that loaf.

MARIANNA: I'm going to make a currant pudding out of it.

PANIA: What are you talking about, pudding? From that fresh loaf?

MARIANNA: That's right – for Shura's farewell dinner.

PANIA: It's a thousand times better than that.

MARIANNA: Better than what, farewell dinners?

PANIA: Stodgy puddings. I only have regular customers, you know.

MARIANNA: All right, I won't come again.

PANIA: I can name a clear dozen that would live off that loaf for a week. They wouldn't throw it away in a pudding.

MARIANNA: Well, I can't give it back to you.

PANIA: Don't worry. I can't have it back...after you've pawed it.

MARIANNA: They probably do put it in puddings, you know.

PANIA: Don't you try telling me about my dear customers. Dear to me, they are. Precious. Why, we've known each other for years. We don't do business with Zhenka Rodin's like.

MARIANNA: You're insulting me, aren't you?

PANIA: You're insulting yourself – Zhenka Rodin. Why should I want to insult you?

MARIANNA: That's just what I'm –

PANIA: I let you in, didn't I? You couldn't be bothered to read the notice, but I let you in anyway. The train broke down, so we had to push it. Then I discovered the delivery was short.

MARIANNA: I thought it must be.

PANIA: But none of that mattered. There you were. 'Here's a woman in trouble', I told myself... '...a woman that's cold, desperate for bread'.

MARIANNA: And I'm very grateful.

PANIA: What more do you want me to do?

MARIANNA: You don't mean that you actually pushed the train?

PANIA: It ran out of diesel – what else could we do?

MARIANNA: No wonder you wanted to open late.

PANIA: You don't have to worry about me. I'm a strong, healthy woman – I'll never go off to the city.

A pause.

MARIANNA: Doesn't little Inna Igorovna work here?

PANIA: What about it?

MARIANNA: I just wondered, that's all.

PANIA: And what about if she works here...what's it to you?

MARIANNA: Is she late?

PANIA: What business is it of yours? I'm warning you – if you've come here to make trouble for Inna...if the two of you are in some kind of feud...

MARIANNA: I'm not out to make any trouble...

PANIA: ...you'll be doing it all on my time. That makes it my business, I suppose. Doesn't it?

MARIANNA: Look, let me...I'm Inna's teacher, all right?

PANIA: She told me she left school.

MARIANNA: Well, that's right. She said she was going to be working here...she recommended you.

PANIA: No, she didn't.

MARIANNA: All right, believe what you want. You will anyway.

PANIA: I believe what Inna herself told me. Why shouldn't I? I'm her mother's best friend.

MARIANNA: How is Zoya Igorovna?

PANIA: Don't pretend like you know her, too.

MARIANNA: I don't at all, but you see I believe you.

PANIA: Oh, you do? Inna tells me she's terrified of you. What do you think of that?

MARIANNA: I don't...I think she didn't.

PANIA: Are you calling me a liar or are you just shocked by the truth? (Running on.) And before you say anything else, I don't want to know anything about it.

MARIANNA (A beat.): What time is she coming in?

PANIA: That doesn't matter – I'm not going to allow you to wait. You got your bread?

MARIANNA: ...and you got your money.

PANIA (Trying to push her out.): ....concluding the business between us...Goodbye.

MARIANNA: Won't you at least...give her a message from me?

PANIA: I'm not getting involved in your squabbles.

MARIANNA: But look...I'm sorry...this is absolutely fantastic to me.

PANIA: I don't give that for what you're telling me. (She makes a Russian gesture signifying 'nothing' – her thumbs between index and middle fingers pointed at the person.)

MARIANNA: But we've had no squabble. It's almost as though you're talking about other people. I'm devoted to Inna Igorovna. I taught her for years. I wanted to see where she works.

PANIA: Why?

MARIANNA: I'm interested in her welfare...we both are.

PANIA: I'm not a charity warden.

MARIANNA: Well, of course not.

PANIA: I'm going to put her to work...she's going to have to work hard.

MARIANNA: I know that – you're giving her a chance. That's why I wanted to meet you.

PANIA: She ought to be working – nearly twenty years old. Does she think she's going to be kept all her life, like a Number One cripple? She's not crippled at all, some would say.

MARIANNA: It's good to hear you talk that way. That's just what she needs.

PANIA: Oh, so you're her employer, are you? Well, she's working for me now – you had your chance.

MARIANNA: Wonderful. I said I'm her teacher.

PANIA: She's unskilled. What on earth could you have taught her, for God's sake – mathematics?

MARIANNA: Art.

PANIA: What – 'art'? Oh-ho-ho. That's not a trade.

MARIANNA: I didn't say it was.

PANIA: So you trained her for nothing. I see.

MARIANNA: I'm not going to argue with you. We'd never get anywhere with it. I just wanted to say –

PANIA: She told me about you and all.

MARIANNA: I'm sure she did. That's where we have common ground.

PANIA: You were the worst form of bully, she said.

MARIANNA: I...beg your pardon?

PANIA: '...bordering on the sadistic...'

MARIANNA *(A beat.)*: I think we must be talking about different people.

PANIA: Those were her very words. Society judged her to be unclean, and you made sure she stayed that way.

MARIANNA: I'd prefer you not to say any more.

PANIA: It's the same girl, though, isn't it. She gave me a graphic account.

MARIANNA: Please don't say any more! I'm sorry that I bothered you. *(Hurt, she starts toward the door.)*

PANIA *(Following after her.)*: In Soviet days, we could send you to prison.

INNA comes on from the back.

INNA: But I never meant Madam Seligman!

MARIANNA: Inna?

PANIA: Eh? You stood where you're now standing and wept it out. Like you're weeping now.

MARIANNA: You make me want to weep.

INNA: But I was talking about the home guardians...not...for a minute...not you.

PANIA: ...and is that why you were terrified when you saw her just now? *(To MARIANNA.)* She ran and hid from you. Now I know why. *(To INNA.)* Now I understand perfectly, my darling.

MARIANNA: Well, I'm afraid I don't. *(To INNA.)* How did I terrify you exactly? Please tell me.

INNA: But you didn't. It's all a –

MARIANNA: Why were you hiding from me? Did I beat you? *(To PANIA.)* I critiqued her artwork – that was my job. *(To INNA.)* Are you upset that I didn't proclaim you a genius? Another Frida Kahlo?

INNA: I'm not upset!

MARIANNA: Go to art school, test yourself out, if you want to find out what you're really worth.

INNA: No...wait a minute...that's what upsets me.

MARIANNA: You confuse interest with instant acclaim.

INNA: No, I don't! Really.

MARIANNA: Kahlo had to wait...years. She lived a virtual lifetime in her husband's shadow. That's the whole point about Kahlo – I told you.

PANIA: Who's this Kahlo you're talking about?

MARIANNA: Woman still-life artist...Mexican...disabled.

PANIA: And that's why she's terrified...another cripple? She's not even Russian. *(To INNA.)* You'll never meet her.

MARIANNA: She died in the 1950s.

PANIA: A dead cripple? *(To MARIANNA.)* I know what this is – guilty conscience. *(Back to INNA.)* You're thinking about your dead comrades, aren't you? *(Then back to MARIANNA.)* She was talking about it today.

MARIANNA: I don't think you quite understand.

INNA: No, she doesn't.

PANIA *(To MARIANNA.):* How do you know? You weren't here. *(To INNA.)* If that's all you've got to worry about... *(To MARIANNA.)* You know what they'd call it in Soviet times, don't you? Morbid self-interest. She'd be judged a State enemy...a pariah.

MARIANNA: She was born a pariah.

PANIA: What do you want me to do about it? In Soviet times, I'd be put under surveillance for even employing such a person, and you're both pointing the finger at me.

MARIANNA: ...because these are different times. And who's pointing the finger? You are!

INNA: ...and you were calling the Pioneers criminals. You didn't like Soviet life.

PANIA: I was talking about bad Pioneers. The Pioneer ideal was beautiful. It's how we lived. And you were excluded – enemy!

INNA: ...because I couldn't walk.

PANIA: So? Complain to your paediatrician – I can't help you.

MARIANNA (*Seizing INNA's arm.*): Come on, darling. I've got the funding to send you to art school.

INNA: No!

MARIANNA: But this is no place at all for you. You heard her just now. I'm not at all sure the misunderstanding wasn't the real truth. (*To PANIA.*) You're the sadist, my dear. That much is perfectly obvious. How could she join the Pioneers?

PANIA: She said it – she didn't.

MARIANNA: So you wanted perfect bodies, like the Germans?

PANIA: They'd have called you a traitor for saying that. You'd have been shot the same day.

MARIANNA: You're living the glorious Soviet myth.

PANIA: Hey, you can't take her out of here.

MARIANNA: I'll pay you her wage, don't you worry.

PANIA: And just who do I get to replace her at this notice? Any minute now they'll be breaking down the door.

MARIANNA: And just how do you think she can help you? You need a strong, healthy girl for work of that kind. Could she push the bread train? You know she couldn't.

INNA: No, all right, but I wanted to.

MARIANNA: Now you're just being ridiculous. You couldn't even lift the bread tray.

INNA: Not the train, I know, or the tray. But the job, yes, the ordinary job.

MARIANNA: ...but not this job.

INNA: Believe it or not, I thought this one, yes. That's why I was frightened to see you, you see – you disapprove.

MARIANNA: It's your life.

PANIA: ...and my shop, if you're sure you don't mind.

MARIANNA: I'm not sure you'll really be happy.

PANIA: Another bourgeois conceit....

INNA: I'm not here to be happy.

PANIA: That's right – she's here to work.

MARIANNA: But you can do so much better.

PANIA: At what – her 'artwork'?

MARIANNA: I can get you a place. *(To PANIA.)* Let her do what she can, yah?

PANIA: She can help me.

MARIANNA: A fit girl would be better...you know it.

PANIA: She'll do for now.

MARIANNA *(To INNA.)*: '...for now', you see? She's no intention whatever of making you permanent.

INNA: And I've no idea I'll be any good.

PANIA: It's time you learned, eh? I was moving heavy machinery when I was half her age.

MARIANNA: That's pure fabrication – we never had child labour.

PANIA: She's bone idle at twenty years old!

MARIANNA: But she's not – that's my point.

PANIA: Oh, no, I forgot – she produces 'art'.

MARIANNA: Others do as well. Why are you so inflexible?

PANIA: I'm a worker.

MARIANNA: And that makes the rest of us what, parasites? I teach. You went to school, didn't you?

PANIA: Not your sort of school.

MARIANNA: That's pure envy.

PANIA: Bourgeois pig. While Russia is starving herself, you produce what – fine *objets d'art*, still-lives of what, exactly? And just what does she produce that you're so anxious to bring forth to the world?

At some point here, the two women tug for INNA.

INNA: Oh, no, please. Both of you.

PANIA: No, really, I'm genuinely interested. I didn't know a Kandinsky walked into my life. Is my shop here all part of your study? You want to do a still-life...an in-depth study of the rat? I'll just try to see where he's gone. I suppose you don't mind – you might even prefer – that he's dead. Yes, it might give your statement more meaning.

MARIANNA: You had industrial art in the thirties.

PANIA: We've no industry! You want to announce to us all life is shitty? We know that already – we can smell our own shit. Are you about to tell us what to do with it to make our life better, is that it? Oh, well, thank you.

MARIANNA: I'm not prepared to have this discussion.

PANIA: I don't discuss things – I told her that.

INNA: Just before you came in.

MARIANNA: That's not the point anyway – it's what Inna herself wants to do.

PANIA: You're wrong – it's what I want in my shop. You came in here wanting my bread.

MARIANNA: I came because of Inna.

PANIA: She's not for sale.

MARIANNA: ...and she's not a commodity.

PANIA: ...that's right – she's pretty well useless.

MARIANNA: Then why don't you just let her go? You're not bothered about keeping her, admit it. You just detest giving in. I've met women like you before. Object on principle.

PANIA: I made a promise to her mother.

MARIANNA: Yah.

PANIA: 'Make her useful, Pania Andreyevna', that's exactly what she said.

MARIANNA: As if either one of you cares either way. Do you know where her mother is now?

PANIA: Finding a job in the city.

MARIANNA: Or she could be halfway to Bryansk. And when is she going to return? Do we know that? If she cared, they'd have gone off together. 'Making her useful' would have sent Inna out to beg. That mother of hers didn't even care enough to exploit her. And you're going to stand there pretending there was ever anything stronger between them than the biological fact?

INNA: Can't you stop this please?

PANIA: There you go upsetting the poor girl – talking that way about her mother.

INNA: Supposing she didn't really care...supposing she's not coming back, for all anyone knows.

PANIA: You let this old witch upset you too much. *(To MARIANNA.)* It's you that wants to exploit her, dear.

INNA: All right, my mother didn't care for me all that much. I know that. It might have been law, but she needn't have sent me away...even if I'm Number One disabled, I'm not helpless. She didn't have to...

PANIA: Don't allow yourself to be deluded – she's a good woman, Zoya Igorovna. She wanted the best for you.

INNA: Do you really know her? Because I never did. My Auntie Yulia paid me more visits than anyone else in the family. It was always my dream to leave to look after her when I was old enough. But then she died. It was only after I left that I discovered the details. She had consumption. No one bothered to tell me. I understand they never gave me a thought. I was fourteen and a half...when they closed down the house, and I went to look for my mother. It wasn't straightforward – I only had one address, I don't remember being there. 'Somewhere outside of Petersburg', someone directed me. I'd never even taken the train. You could say I was like a young colt...my first steps of freedom. I saw a moving staircase, going down. I'd never been on one, and I was plainly terrified...All those people...I thought I'd be trampled to death once I tried. And suddenly I wished I was back at the home. I started to cry, and I heard people round me, shouting, 'Who is she?' 'What's she done?' 'Somebody had better get hold of a policeman'...as though I'd committed a crime!

PANIA: There – you see? She'd be lost by herself in the city. You heard her say it – trampled to death.

Gradually, for this account, INNA becomes 'able-bodied' – to the point of rebounding from side to side like a rubber ball.

INNA: ...somebody suddenly took hold of my arm...I thought at first a policeman...and that I'd be taken off, thrown in detention somewhere...or worse...down the moving staircase. But no, he was moving us to the open air, doing it in such a way I found...gentle. He asked me where I was headed, and I heard myself saying automatically, 'The train for Settlement Number 7.' So we got in a taxi, then into a train...I fell asleep from the motion...only to find when I woke up – he'd delivered me to my mother's door. I think before I fell asleep he told me his name was Pavel Zakharin. Did I dream it? He volunteered that his father had been a general in the Patriotic War. I think I went to sleep believing, 'We're not likely to get lost then.' And...oh, yes, I think he made me eat a supper of brown bread, buttermilk and radishes...She wasn't unhappy to see me, my mother. We embraced...then she put me to bed. And I know I was dreaming this time...about a moving staircase...and the dormitory at the home. But in this dream the general's son turned out to be Yekaterina Olmyoskaia, the last matron we had at the home. It was her face I saw when I woke up next morning, though of course it was my mother's voice. 'It's 7.00, and I've made rice porridge if you're hungry, and then you'd better get ready for school.' That's when I knew that my new life had begun, and that I was bound to survive.

PANIA (To MARIANNA.): And you were her teacher, I suppose.

MARIANNA: Only one of them, though I think I was probably the one that most cared.

INNA: I felt I was always your favourite...I always wanted to ask why.

PANIA: Jews always want to mother everybody. (To MARIANNA.) Was your daughter at home at the time?

MARIANNA (To INNA.): You never reminded me of Shura, but I thought of Kahlo, I admit, straightaway. And that painting by Velasquez – the group portrait with the little girl who's adored by the dwarf.

INNA: You've shown me a photograph of it.

MARIANNA: The aristocracy always looked after their lame ones...like beloved family pets. It wasn't looked on as misfortune to be lame.

PANIA: Here, she's an act at the circus, so what?

MARIANNA: I want to look after you, darling.

INNA: I know that, Marianna.

PANIA: And did you happen to hear what else she said? She doesn't want that...she's afraid of the city, for one thing. And, for another, she's no liking for being a 'family pet'.

INNA: That's not it either.

PANIA: Why is it you're always arguing with me?

MARIANNA: You're speaking for her...

PANIA: ...and you're sending her back where she came. Where's the sense in that?

MARIANNA (To INNA.): You know that's not true. (A beat.) I'm giving her the chance of a career.

INNA: Perhaps next year.

MARIANNA: They won't hold the place. And how do you know you wouldn't be able to cope on your own? You spent an afternoon, when you'd just been released. What kind of test is that?

INNA: You expect me to go from that straight to living on my own.

MARIANNA: It's six years later, and you're not on your own. You'd be living with Shura.

INNA: But she doesn't know me. You expect her to look after someone she doesn't even know...a –

MARIANNA: Don't you dare use the word 'cripple'.

INNA: ... 'total stranger' I was going to say. She'd expect me at least to contribute.

MARIANNA: And so you would...why not?

INNA: You don't know that, Marianna.

MARIANNA: Better than you do yourself.

PANIA: There, you see? You want to do her living for her.

INNA: It's not that I don't think I would contribute or make my own friends...

MARIANNA: Shura's a good girl...responsible.

INNA: No, but she didn't adopt me, did she. *(A beat.)* Can't we stay as we are?

MARIANNA: And how's that, exactly? You're not still at school.

INNA: We can still see each other.

MARIANNA *(Disappointed.)*: Yah, sure.

INNA: It's better this way...you'll see. *(Moving toward her.)* I know my limitations, better than anyone else, which is natural.

MARIANNA: So you want to be a lone wolf, a pariah, as our friend said.

INNA: I only wish I could make you understand.

MARIANNA: You wish to persuade me. I understand very well.

INNA: It's only because of my condition.

MARIANNA: It's the condition of Russia, my dear. People become friends with their condition... they depend on it, finally become enslaved by it. Like the people in this village.

PANIA: I'll give you 'enslaved', all right.

MARIANNA: You do nothing, quite frankly, to help yourselves.

PANIA: No, of course. We just moved a whole bloody train. Of course, that's no match at all for talking about art and culture and civilisation. Move mountains you do with your talk, I forgot.

MARIANNA: You make me sound like a Pre-Revolutionary.

PANIA: An Anti-Revolutionary, sure.

MARIANNA: Stop living in the past. *(A beat.)* I don't blame you entirely, either of you. My daughter insists she knows better than I do.

INNA: But you want her to go to the city...don't you?

MARIANNA: I only want her to live, to act right. She convinced me to send her to Germany, to study architecture. What happens? She comes back a year later, no qualification, no job, of course. And she asked for the place for herself.

INNA: She's got to have it, of course – she's your birth daughter. I'm glad you told me.

MARIANNA: But she doesn't deserve it...as you do, if only you've sense enough.

INNA: She's your daughter...you're both artists. You can't ask me to replace her in your life.

MARIANNA: I never said anything like that.

INNA: You did without realising it, through your actions. That's not fair to any of us, dear.

MARIANNA: What can you possibly know about it?

INNA: Not a thing, in specifics. We've never met. But I'd want my own mother to care. (*Moving toward her.*) Make it up with her, Marianna, before you lose her for good. She's asking that of you. I know it.

PANIA: I know it and all. She has to want more than a mouldy bread pudding.

MARIANNA: And there's nothing I can do to persuade you...you're determined to fight your own battles.

INNA: I'll be thinking of you, though, more than you could know. (*Choking back the tears.*) I'm ever so glad we had this chance to...

MARIANNA: That's precisely what disturbs me. (*As she goes out.*) Make sure you don't turn her into the family cat – you'll skin her and eat her alive.

She goes off.

PANIA: That's a marvellous thought, isn't it?

INNA: She's really a generous person.

PANIA: That daughter of hers is a whore.

INNA: What?

PANIA: That's what she's gone to the city to do. I've seen her round the place, looking for clients.

INNA: I'm sure you're mistaken.

PANIA: That shitheel Zhenka Rodin – he's the one. Mafia agent, he arranged for her transfer. That's what you were headed for, my deluded darling. Tonight, as you play with your finger paints, please reflect on your avoided fate.

INNA: I'm sure that's not true. Marianna would have to know.

PANIA: I could tell at once she's a fool. You did exactly the right thing to send her packing. I can just hear her moaning into the night, 'Oh, why have I been so forsaken', because she's such an idiot. That's exactly what she deserves. *(She surveys the state of her shop – loaves still on the trays.)* And here, look. We haven't managed to do a thing with these...all through entertaining your friends. That's where indulging the arts gets you.

Someone else – this time a man – is outside the door.

OSIP: Madame Pania Andreyevna!

INNA: Shall I open up for him?

PANIA: In your babyfat dreams – we're through entertaining for one day!

OSIP: I've got something I need to discuss with you.

PANIA: That did it – discussion is out, just like he is...and he's going to stay that way.

INNA: He could be a customer.

PANIA: All right, you tell him to fuck a donkey – let's see what you're made of.

INNA: Well, I'm hardly likely, am I...to tell him that. *(Crosses to the door and calls out.)* We're not open yet...Can you come back in...half an hour?

OSIP: I'm not a customer, tell her.

INNA: Oh, dear. Aren't you?

PANIA *(Through the door.)*: Then don't bother returning at all! *(To INNA.)* Did you happen to tell all your friends?

INNA: I don't know who it is.

OSIP: I'm here, as you might say, 'officially'. That is, on business...urgent business. Well, I'm here anyway.

This compels PANIA to peek through a window to see who it is.

PANIA: Oh, God...Osip Pishchik.

INNA: Is he a regular?

PANIA: Regular pain in the arse, yeah. I forgot to warn you about him.

INNA: Warn me – what about?

PANIA (*Through the door.*): No delivery today, sweetheart....back to beddy-byes with you.

OSIP: Is that you, Pania dear?

PANIA: Can you remember where your bed is?

OSIP: I'm not here about bread!

PANIA: Not 'bread', dear, I said bed – your bed. You shouldn't have left it so early.

OSIP: Of course, I'll buy bread, if that's what you want. You're in business yourself, I know. You can't afford to let a working moment go by without profit. I'll add to that profit, if I can.

PANIA:Can you hear me at all? There's no bread today. The bastards forgot to deliver.

OSIP: ...but I still need to speak to you.

PANIA: Shall I send for your friend Volkov...the Inspector? Would that fill you with comfort and joy?

OSIP: Volkov, you say? That's very funny.

PANIA: We can ask him to put you to bed, if you want.

OSIP: No, I don't think we want Volkov just yet. Of course, he'll have to be in on it at some time or other.

PANIA: Then I'd leave, if I was you, before he appears on the scene.

OSIP: No, I've got to see you first, dear...for your own good.

PANIA (*To INNA.*): You'd be having to deal with this sooner or later. Just as well you see it now.

INNA: Osip Pishchik? But I do know him. He doesn't bother you, does he?

PANIA: Pain in the arse.

INNA: That surprises me, because I always thought he was –

PANIA: He's one of the ones they ought to clear out. They would do it, no problem, in Soviet times...

INNA: If you mean what I think –

PANIA: I mean 'imprison' or 'hospitalize'...get rid of anyway.

INNA: Then I'm afraid I can't agree.

PANIA: You've only just come out yourself.

INNA: ...from the home, not from prison...and it was four or five years ago. It was a kind of a prison.

PANIA: I know what I meant. Too sheltered to know that people like Pishchik exist, and you've got to deal with them the best way you can.

INNA: What do you mean? I've known people like Pishchik...I've known Pishchik. I think he's nice...I think you should let him in.

PANIA: And I think you're crazy.

INNA: Well, as you say – it's your shop. I'm only the shopgirl...and this is only my first day.

PANIA: And we've had one interruption already.

INNA: My friend Marianna. Yes, that's very true.

PANIA: So would you please let me deal with this?

INNA: I just think you're being unfair...all right – fire me.

PANIA: I just want you to shut up a minute.

INNA: If I could perhaps talk with him? There's no need at all for police.

She starts to unlock the door.

PANIA: Once he gets in, we'll never get rid of him...ourselves.

INNA: Oh, we won't need 'to get rid of him' at all. He came to the home all the time. He did magic tricks for us. Then he...went away again.

PANIA: Wait a minute. *(Hand against the door.)* What do you mean he did tricks for you?

INNA: Magic tricks. He made us all laugh. Of course, we were only about eight or nine...they probably wouldn't amuse me now.

PANIA: (He's worse than I thought.) What else did he do?

INNA: Told us stories? I forget. That's probably because he wasn't that good at storytelling.

PANIA: Did he touch you at all? Did those freaks let him handle you?

INNA: What 'freaks'? What are you on about?

PANIA: Those guardians you say were like sadists...that made a habit of handling you...did they let people like Pishchik –

INNA: Why do you say, 'people like Pishchik'? No one did anything to us!

PANIA: So what were you talking about earlier?

INNA: Neglect, I was saying – not that.

PANIA: Do you understand – ?

INNA: I know. Chikatilo. I'm not stupid.

PANIA: But you could have forgotten...They say –

INNA: Well, they're wrong. It was only ten years ago, in my very young – so you're telling me – life. I forgot nothing at all about their care...Pishchik did nothing like what you're talking about. I'd have known, wouldn't I?

PANIA: What were they doing letting him in?

INNA: I told you – he did tricks. Maybe they thought they wouldn't have to work the time he was there. I dunno. But I can tell you how it happened. He'd bribe them. That's clear enough, isn't it? Nobody anywhere has enough money. He paid them to let him entertain us. I remember, because the first time he said he came from my village...and I thought maybe he was related to me in some way...maybe married to Auntie Yulia. He didn't come very often anyway...not more than two or three times...

PANIA: All right, if he didn't do anything, who else – ?

INNA: I don't want to talk about...it's rubbish, okay? No one did anything to us. We lived a fairy tale.

OSIP (Singing it.): I'm still wait-ing/ Pania Andry-ov-na! (Speaking it.) I'm still here.

INNA: I thought he must have died or moved away.

PANIA: And aren't you thrilled now he's never done either?

OSIP now launches into the beginning of 'March of the Aviators'.

OSIP: 'We were born to make fairy tales come true...'

PANIA (To INNA.): Did he ever do that at the home?

She now moves to open the door.

OSIP: '...We have steel wings for arms!' (Almost falling through the door.) Hello, my dear. (Seeing INNA.) And who's this...? No! It can't be...it's little Inyechka!

INNA (Tentatively.): Hello, Osip Pishchik.

OSIP: You're a butterfly now – a speckled yellow for sure.

We now see he's a shambling 50-year-old.

INNA: I wasn't sure you'd remember me...once Pania Andreyevna said –

OSIP: Why, it's only been a few years. And you're a living portrait now, aren't you...a tiny masterpiece.

PANIA: Let's leave it before you get overwhelmed by the artwork. We had one exhibition already.

INNA: I hope you're all right.

OSIP: Me? Oh, yes, fine, should I say indestructible, why? Did you imagine I'd died?

INNA: I've thought of you very often, in fact...I missed you.

OSIP: Oh, don't say that.

INNA: But it's quite true.

OSIP: That breaks my heart, you know? Because I never went back to see you. I did try one or two years ago. But then they said the home had been closed down.

INNA: It was more than two years ago....more like five.

OSIP: Is it as long as that? Those poor little kiddykins.

PANIA: All right, stop it. She works here now. What do you want, bread?

OSIP: Do you want me to have it?

PANIA: I want you to say what you want and then go...I don't want you hanging round. You can see Inna later – another time and a very large distance from here, please.

OSIP: I love meeting Inna again, of course – instantly I'm a young man. But it's you, my dear Pania Andreyevna, that I've come to see...on a personal matter, you understand? A bit delicate, a bit personal.

INNA: I'll leave the room.

PANIA: You stay right there. He doesn't know me 'personally'.

OSIP: What, not know you? I've known you since schooldays.

PANIA: Oh, yeah?

OSIP: It's perfectly true we've not seen so much of each other in recent years. But I assure you, I remember the day you organized the cleaning when the janitors were snowbound after that job at Settlement 32. *(For INNA's benefit.)* Our school had been closed the previous month, and, somehow, it hadn't been cleaned. The teachers – well, you can imagine – were beside themselves – there was no ground staff, and the state of the toilets alone left us shocked. But your fearless employer there... *(To PANIA.)* ...you took it all on yourself, didn't you, dear. You looked Principal Comrade Luzhkov straight in the eye, and you said, 'Don't worry, Comrade Principal, we'll have it spotless overnight'! And you did, didn't you, working away through the night. It was as though we'd never been closed. You saved the ground staff their jobs, didn't you? I remember thinking at the time, 'This one is destined for leadership, no doubt.'

PANIA: Yeah? And now look where I am.

OSIP: And the school numbered two or three hundred...it wasn't small. It must have taken most of the night, yes, to clean.

INNA: This morning she helped push the bread train.

OSIP: Who could doubt it? Wings of steel, you see? Even now. You're in the most capable hands you could find. She won't fail you. Overnight, the entire school. Four whole storeys.

PANIA: I'm not impressed.

INNA: You're too modest.

PANIA: You want something, Osip Yegorovich. You didn't come here to reflect on my glory.

OSIP: I came to warn you.

PANIA: ...of what?

INNA: Something to do with the shortage, I bet.

PANIA: I know all about that...see? That's all they sent. Do you want a white loaf? *(Proffering loaf.)* Here, take it...and go. Get out, go. *(Tries to push him out the door.)*

OSIP: I discovered a body...late last night.

PANIA: Yes, I know – the body of your great grandfather...He appeared to you out of the mists of time.

OSIP: No, I think it's your husband, in fact.

PANIA: Fuck off.

INNA: You really shouldn't joke like that, Mr Osip.

OSIP: Dear me, did you think I was joking?

INNA: Well, I hoped you were.

PANIA: I think he's plain wrong – drunk, deluded, missing a few of your marbles. I told her to be on her guard.

OSIP: I don't doubt it sounds strange to you – unexpected and therefore a shock. You're probably wondering if you heard right...and once it hits you, no doubt, there will be grief. Had you known each other very long, say, from schooldays?

PANIA: You found no body!

INNA: Denial, that is. Marianna told me. It's what they now call being in denial. She says I'm in denial about my condition, but that that's a good thing. Usually it's said of something...not so good.

OSIP: Of course, I can't be sure it's his body or not. But you should take a look.

PANIA (*Physical contact.*): Can you see me, old man? Are you listening to me? My husband's not dead, and there's no body no place. It's just a figment of your deluded...your warped mind...and I've got a day's work ahead of me. I was out there pushing a bloody bread train at 4.00 in the morning.

OSIP: You should have a little lie-down first, of course.

PANIA: I'll lie down, all right. I'll lie you down, lay you out, I'll flatten you blin-style, how's that? Idiot.

OSIP: I'm not for a moment suggesting you murdered him.

PANIA: Next time I'll murder you, no problem.

OSIP: But you've got to admit to yourself the possibility, the mere possibility –

PANIA: Will you kindly shut up?

OSIP: ...like, for instance, he's not at home, and he hasn't been home for a matter of –

INNA: ...three or four months. Isn't that what you told me?

PANIA: You can shut up and all. Whose side are you on?

INNA: Oh, I'm not suggesting it either. But I don't think Mr Osip would lie or make a mistake like that. I definitely think there's been –

PANIA: You definitely nothing-on-earth. You can't move to use public transport. I told you he went to the city. If you don't believe me –

INNA: My memory is that he could be anywhere. Bryansk was one place you mentioned.

PANIA: It doesn't matter, all right? Because I know where he is and the whore he's shacked up with, all right? Got the picture?

INNA (*A beat.*): You still ought to see the body.

OSIP: I think Pania Andreyevna wants to give herself time to adjust.

INNA: When, exactly, did you discover – ?

OSIP: Late last night, early this morning.

INNA: And, exactly, what state was it in?

OSIP: Well, I'm hardly what you'd call expert. I mean an expert could determine everything, possibly immediately. All I saw was a male – snow-covered, of course, in weather like this...

INNA: And half-eaten by wolves?

OSIP: What?

INNA: I mean...could he have starved, possibly?

OSIP: Quite possibly, yes, though I wouldn't like to venture offhand. But wolves? Where'd you get that idea?

PANIA: From the storybook, like you did.

OSIP: People have died through the ages in such circumstances. You can't deny that, dear.

PANIA: They've also been shot in battle...they die of plague, rare diseases and heart failure. How does that affect me?

INNA: Did he meet with a violent death, do we know? Did you see blood?

PANIA: Perhaps he was still breathing...gasping for life...and you walked away from the scene. Perhaps we can hold you responsible.

OSIP: I'm fully prepared to tell what I know...and leave my judgement to God.

PANIA: Oh, that's that then – you'll burn in hell. (Sighs.) That's a load off my mind anyway.

INNA: Why so reluctant to believe, Pania Andreyevna? Where does it profit Mr Osip?

OSIP: It's true, you know – I came here as an article of faith, of friendship, though we've always been a bit distant. I always thought you disapproved of me, for some reason I never knew.

PANIA: No reason, eh?

OSIP: No, I never knew it, that's all. It's been a complete mystery to me ever since –

PANIA: Because we never knew each other at school or anywhere else. There you are – mystery solved.

OSIP: Of course we did. There's only one school in the village. It's perfectly true we weren't in the same classroom together...I'm a year or two older than you are.

PANIA: Ten years and you're just barely literate. *(To INNA.)* That janitor nonsense he vomited up? Pure invention. You can add 'fraud' to his list of unforgettable attributes.

OSIP: I respect and admire you deeply.

PANIA: You accuse me of murder, that's what.

OSIP: I only talked about a body in the snow.

PANIA: ...and there's bodies of chickens and dogs as well as, occasionally, human remains. What gave you the notion I'd be interested? Am I a...what is it now...taxiderm?

OSIP: It's a short distance only from here. We'd definitely have to say circumstantial.

PANIA: Circumstantial of what?

INNA: Maybe someone's heart gave out when you were moving the train.

PANIA: We'd have recovered it...sent for the doctor. *(To OSIP.)* Well? I'm waiting.

OSIP: I'll tell you...everything I know. He was already dead...dunno how many hours...but half-buried beneath the latest drift.

PANIA: How enlightening! And what does Volkov say about the matter?

OSIP: Volkov?

PANIA: Village constable, yes. *(To INNA.)* Watch closely now. *(To OSIP.)* You naturally first thought of contacting him, the man in charge.

OSIP: No, frankly, I didn't.

PANIA *(To INNA.)*: Shit-laden scared of him, see? *(To OSIP.)* You didn't? Wasn't that naughty of you?

OSIP: I thought first of the Mafia.

PANIA: Oh, I see, yes, the –

OSIP: ...Mafia, yes, of a Mafia hit. Things have gone seriously wrong in recent times in this village. *(To INNA.)* I tremble for you when I think of the world you're being reborn into. Though things couldn't have been all that pleasant in your place of confinement, the world we've come to know now is not the same one we've known for years. Cases of perversion were once isolated, perhaps even removed altogether. Harder, yes, there was a finality. But absolute outcomes served absolute values as well – absolutely. Now what there is is a corruption they're calling 'a necessary'. Necessary what, of course, no one says. *(To PANIA.)* I half-thought that Volkov was mixed up in it, see?

PANIA: Oh, but surely you trust Volkov, don't you? You must have known him at school.

OSIP *(Whispers.)*: You can keep a secret?

PANIA *(Playing along.)*: Yes, what is it?

OSIP: I will tell him, yes, but in my own time. *(Whispers.)* It's all part of my plan to trap him.

PANIA: Congratulations.

OSIP: I'll know how far he's involved by his reactions, you see. I'll assume his complete innocence straight away. Then I'll assume that he's squarely involved – his own man did it. And I'll determine the truth from his reaction to my forthright declaration: 'I found a body in the snow!'

PANIA: Lunatic.

INNA: I think that's very sound.

PANIA: You're both lunatics. *(Yawns.)* It's not yet 8.00...and I've been up for a day and a half... another full day ahead. You want nourishment? Here, take it in both hands. *(Pushing bread in OSIP'S direction.)* Somebody died, and there's not enough bread. Early winter – there's not enough fuel. Nobody has enough money, so they barter their lives away...or they thieve. Twenty-five possible reasons why people die before their time. Don't come to me with your revelations – you don't even have a decent roof. So now tell me – did you do it yourself for the money?

OSIP: You...what?

PANIA: I'm not thinking Mafia money – you're just broke. Haven't eaten for two or three days, for one thing.

INNA: Wait a minute. First you didn't believe him...

PANIA: I'm just showing how easy it is. *(To OSIP.)* Why come to me...why not the authorities?

OSIP: I told you – he seemed to resemble your husband.

PANIA: What does that mean? You were a friend of his...you were anxious to see justice done?

OSIP: Well, no, as a matter of fact, I heard you'd hired a disabled girl...and I wanted to see if it was the girl that I knew from long ago.

PANIA: And what's that to do with the body?

OSIP: Body?

PANIA: That you say you found, that's right.

OSIP: Oh, well, I thought that his face looked familiar....

PANIA: We're back to him now, are we?

OSIP: ...and I knew that you keep a shotgun in back.

PANIA: Sounds a situation ripe for blackmail. You may remember, I've been asking what it is you want.

OSIP: ...all right, now, I've been asking you for nothing at all, except maybe your trust. That hunter of yours has tongues wagging...people are saying it's extreme...woman in your situation, a village fixture.

PANIA: The extremity is the bread shortage – people shortly become desperate.

INNA: I'm sure you just mean it as a precaution – you wouldn't actually assault anyone.

PANIA: I'm a woman alone in this 'extreme situation'.

OSIP: Yes, and people are wondering aloud about that. They wonder all sorts of things.....they always have. 'Why is she alone? She needn't be...she wasn't, we thought. What, exactly, is going on? Where is her husband? And what about this shotgun of hers...?'

INNA: ...that she calls her hunter.

OSIP: People are apt to be inventive when they don't really know for sure.

PANIA: It's none of people's fucking business...or yours. Do you hear me? You think you're all spies...that we're still in the Soviet era...you inform at will and gain preferment. All that's finished, or hadn't you heard? There's nothing to gain from it now – Russia has nothing whatever to give. You want bread – here it is. Take what you can of it. (She begins tossing loaves.) You think you smell blood somewhere? So did I – across the tracks...early morning – the shocking appearance of a dead elephant! Its neck was broken, its head was severed from its body, like a broken toy...all except for the fresh elephant blood that came gushing out like a fountain!

INNA: Oh, please, don't go on about it. *(Turning her head away.)* Oy.

PANIA: Don't be squeamish, dear – it's an excellent basis for your still-life examination of the elementary. You can't afford to turn away. A mere hunter can't account for such carnage. Besides, a hunter – both weapon and man – always makes such a clean kill. This was mutilation in the extreme...and she missed it – compounded tragedy.

OSIP: She lives with her own mutilation, poor darling. You can't blame her.

PANIA: What you mean is she's always been protected from real life. Her friend said as much – she's like a pet, a child's toy. If she's broken by everyday circumstances, she gets thrown away. That's the way it works now. If you can't afford a replacement, you steal or you do completely without. Children outgrow their toys anyway. Only idiots keep them as artefacts. The rest of us settle for real life. *(To INNA.)* You want to go with him to see the body, dear?

INNA: I...only suggested that you might.

PANIA: What on earth for? I've just got back from an elephant shoot! That's enough for one morning in peacetime.

INNA: What's the point of seeing anyway? I never knew your husband.

PANIA: ...whereas I did, you're saying... naturally enough.

INNA: Well, you could identify the body if necessary.

PANIA: What would I need to identify him for? That's not the murder in question. And I wouldn't be guilty if it was. I didn't need to kill him, can you understand that? No? He was dead to me already...through his child.

INNA: What are you talking about, Pania?

PANIA: Oh, for God's sake now, what do you think? And you try to convince me you're not Barbie Doll innocent. You'll have to try harder, that's all. *(To OSIP.)* Hey, you, granddad – this is my confession, don't you want it?

OSIP: No, you misunderstand – I never said you did it.

PANIA: Congratulations. I didn't need to – I'd murdered his child.

OSIP: I supported you right the way along.

INNA *(Relieved.)*: For a minute there I...didn't know what to think.

PANIA: All it was, if you really want it, was that I found out the night after he left that I'd be having his kid if I kept it to term. Well, I also found out that I really wasn't bothered that he left...so what would I want with a daily reminder of him for the next twenty years. There's your murder.

INNA (*Impulsively.*): Oh, dear Pania Andreyevna!

She embraces and kisses her repeatedly.

PANIA: What? We've got all this work to do, what? You want us to play with your dolls?

INNA goes down on her knees to recover the strewn loaves.

INNA: Oh, I'll work for you, don't worry. I'll work hard. Every day I'll get up and think, 'I'm going off to work now...and isn't it fantastic?'

PANIA: All right, you don't have to get on the floor.

INNA: Oh, but it needs to be done...it's soon time to open. And I can, you see? I'm perfectly supple. I'm that much younger than you are, and now I can see that you need me. Oh, how you've suffered in life. I can see what they mean now – Pania Andreyevna, the Bread Lady. What a glorious thing to be needed for life!

PANIA: All right, you'll be sounding like him in a minute...and then I really will start to worry.

OSIP: I need you, too, Inna Igorovna.

INNA: You...what?

OSIP: I love you, my little Inyechka. You're my ideal, you are!

INNA: Oh, no, for...I'm sure you're mistaken, Mr Osip.

The revelation upsets INNA so that her spasticity becomes particularly uncoordinated. Her movements are not unlike those of a trapped butterfly.

OSIP: Oh, now, you've taken a spill. (*Crosses to her.*) This is my fault...let me help you up. You've suffered far more than the rest of us.

INNA: Oh, no, I haven't at all. I'm not at all what you think. Pania Andreyevna, please make it clear to him...I can get up...I'm far better doing it by myself.

There's some physical awkwardness between the two of them before PANIA crosses to sort out the tangle.

PANIA: One's as helpless as the other ... and you're both making a pigsty of my shop. Out of the way, old man. Go on. Get on out of it. You think she wants to hear you drool? And what would people think if they came in right now? 'She doesn't know the first thing about keeping a shop.' They'd think I was giving looters an absolute invitation...and then I'd lose all my stock.

OSIP: No, I don't think you understand.

PANIA: I understand people, all right. The basic ingredients don't change all that much – what's there to understand?

OSIP: But I tell you...I love her...I want us to marry.

INNA: Oh, my God.

OSIP: Yes, I'm sorry, my darling, for not telling you first...for telling her before I told you. There it is, though...it can't be avoided.

INNA: But I don't love you...I mean, I don't know you. I haven't seen you since childhood, have I...you're something sweet from my childhood.

PANIA: You mean he's ridiculous...a clown.

OSIP: You don't know me at all. *(Of INNA.)* She knows.

INNA: Yes, I'm sure you're a very good person.

OSIP: I've kept myself pure.

PANIA: Ha!

INNA: I'm sure of it. I can see it in your eyes. You can always read a person from their eyes... and your character...your smile begins in your eyes...that's a beautiful sign.

OSIP: I knew him, you see...the...the general's son.

INNA: What?

OSIP: The man that brought you here from the home...reunite you with your mother...I knew him personally. He was a personal friend.

INNA: Pavel Zakharin?

OSIP: That's it – Zakharin. He was your guardian angel that day.

INNA: I feel now that you must have known him. I'm glad you told me...especially glad now that we've met again.

OSIP: Fate – that's what it is. God's will. And I'll be your guardian angel hereafter.

PANIA: I've had enough of this.

She moves to force him out the front door, but OSIP suddenly discovers his reserve and stands his ground.

OSIP: You leave me alone...you hear me? We're conversing in unfathomed depth.

INNA: I'm still your friend...I look forward to knowing you again. But it's like I tried to tell my friend Marianna. I need to move on my own first...learn who I am in the world. I've been sheltered all my life, really sheltered.

OSIP: She's an angel.

INNA: I'm nothing like that. I couldn't get on the metro myself at the age when Pania Andreyevna was tractor driving. I'll never drive a tractor, all right. But I am good for something in the world. I must be. God's given me the chance that He didn't give all the others. I've got to try it for them as well...for us all...for the future of us all.

OSIP (Focused on INNA but addressing PANIA.): All that...and you think she's 'unclean'!

PANIA: I never said that...I said you were...

OSIP: What do you know about it anyway? You haven't understood a word of what she's saying.

PANIA: I understand she needs to work.

OSIP: She needs to be recognized for what she is.

PANIA (To INNA.): Oh, God, now he's saying you're divine.

OSIP: That's right...she is – a message from God for the nation.

PANIA (To INNA.): And you think this is what the President meant in his speech? That's where sex leads you, my darling, right there, to him.

INNA: I'm sure everything with him is as it should be.

PANIA: What's that? Do you have any idea? Is it icon worship he's after? He might have you believing...you're for all the ages...that you're older than he is – the dirty young man.

INNA: I think you're being hugely unfair.

PANIA: And I say he's hugely indecent. Has he exposed himself yet? Do we have to wait till he starts exposing himself? He's been stalking you for years...magic roundabouts.

OSIP: You want to leave what doesn't concern you alone.

PANIA: I'm well inside the law here – sexual assault. I could fire on your assets and no one would say I'd done wrong.

INNA: Oh, no, I beseech you both...anything at all except that. (Tearfully, she gets hold of PANIA and wants OSIP to leave for his own sake.) You've got to believe that she means it.

OSIP (Joyous.): Let her, let her...let her draw a bead. You and me are indestructible!

INNA: Oh, my God, how did this happen?

OSIP (Starting off.): Never give it another moment's worry – I'll see you tonight after work.

VOLKOV comes on, blocking OSIP'S retreat. He is a typical officer – ex-military, sadistic, here dressed in a formal overcoat and fur hat.

VOLKOV: You're out very early this morning, Pishchik.

PANIA: Oh, I was beginning to think you'd never get here.

VOLKOV: Don't worry – I've been trailing him for hours. (To OSIP.) Why? What have you been up to?

OSIP: What? It's bread day...wanted to get here early.

VOLKOV: Wanted to be the first one, eh?

PANIA: That's a lie for a start – he said he didn't want bread.

VOLKOV: And it's not bread day on the slag heap, is it.

OSIP: I watched the train coming in...watched them pushing the train. You ask her...ask Pania Andreyevna. There were fifteen of you, weren't there, dear.

VOLKOV: And you'd have us believe you were that – what, hungry? – that you stood watching them all that time.

PANIA: You didn't offer to help, did you? Bastard!

VOLKOV: Oh, well, I expect he had other things on his mind. More important things.

PANIA: Fifteen fair to ageing and infirm women. Lazy bastard.

VOLKOV: Why don't you tell us what those important things were?

PANIA: He came in here all fired up about a body. Lunatic bastard.

VOLKOV: A body, eh?

PANIA: ...specifically, the dead body of a certain man.

VOLKOV: Are you talking about a human corpse?

OSIP: I found it...just lying there.

VOLKOV: And so you came in here and frightened these women about it?

OSIP *(To PANIA.)*: I didn't frighten you, did I? Tell him the truth.

PANIA: Of course, I was frightened. He came in here babbling about –

INNA: I wasn't the least bit frightened, and I'm sure he meant no harm. I knew him from childhood, for one thing.

VOLKOV: But how is it he made his way in here? That in itself is suspicious... *(To OSIP.)* ...isn't it? You seek the police if you find a body...that's anyone's first thought, their first impulse almost, in such a situation. To seek an alternative, well, that needs looking into.

OSIP: All right, don't worry – I'll show you the body. You can't intimidate me.

VOLKOV: I'm not trying to intimidate anybody – I'm just after the truth.

OSIP: We're all after the truth...in our own way.

VOLKOV: And you were thinking, were you, of maybe taking over my job?

OSIP: Why did you follow me? Intimidation.

VOLKOV: Well...you wander the streets at night...up on slag heaps, with corpses. You think that's normal behaviour?

OSIP: You've never caught me at anything, have you?

VOLKOV: There's always a first time...Go home to bed. That's where normal people are at this hour. *(Restraining hand.)* Not now. You've got some explaining to do.

PANIA: And there's a little matter of sexual habits.

INNA: No, there isn't.

PANIA: You stay out of it this time, dear. We've known this species a lot longer than you.

INNA: But you don't know that about him – I refuse to believe...

PANIA: That's right – he didn't declare himself wildly just now...propose 'marriage' to you? I must have misheard.

INNA: You misunderstood anyway. He didn't mean marriage.

OSIP: What else do you think I meant?

INNA: Oh, my God, don't say that. *(To VOLKOV.)* I knew him when I was a child, you see, sir.

VOLKOV: What's he been doing with children?

PANIA: There – you see? What did I tell you?

INNA: He can't tell anything from that. *(To VOLKOV.)* He did magic tricks for us.

PANIA:...in a cripples' home he bribed the guardians to exploit with his 'magic tricks'.

INNA: I tell you he never touched us!

PANIA: ...and I say he's got her spooked.

OSIP: And I've loved you ever since.

INNA: Oh, no!

VOLKOV: That's good enough for me.

VOLKOV now moves on OSIP, while INNA still tries to reason.

INNA: You mustn't say things like that, Mr Osip – it isn't....people don't understand.

VOLKOV: You hear what she said, 'Mr Osip'? It isn't nice...it just isn't done. You shouldn't say things like that...and you certainly can't be allowed to do anything. We've got to see to it that you don't.

With each stressed word, VOLKOV squeezes OSIP'S testicles harder, and INNA'S sobbing increases.

INNA: Let him go...can't you see...oh, please stop it, he didn't do anything. *(To PANIA.)* My God, can't you see what you started? You've got to tell him to stop! *(Hanging onto VOLKOV.)* You've got to stop this!

VOLKOV *(Breathless.)*: All right...I've stopped. I've stopped him and all. He won't do anything to anyone from now on. He's no danger to anyone.

INNA *(Sobbing.)*: He never was.

VOLKOV: You really know nothing about him, dear. He's a menace. They all are, people like him.

INNA: I don't care. I don't care what you say I don't know. I want you to leave him alone, all right? Just leave him.

VOLKOV: I can't do that, dear. He's got to come with me...for his own protection if nothing else.

INNA: Yes, I've heard what you do for people's 'own protection'.

PANIA: Don't be a little fool...you want to anger him against you?

VOLKOV: It's all right. *(To INNA.)* I can't ignore the charges against him, sweetheart.

INNA: Charges? I'm not making any charges. She's not either, are you?

VOLKOV: I'm talking about the vagrancy...I mean, look at him, dear. He's disgusting. Do you really think we can have that disturbing people's – ?

INNA: All right, I'm just like him – a menace – you'd better arrest me as well.

PANIA: I told you to keep your mouth shut.

INNA: Ask Pania Andreyevna what I'm talking about. She knows I was judged a pariah..... unclean. They locked me up for years, too.

VOLKOV: I know that in Soviet times...

INNA: What makes these times any better? Turning on him? What's he ever done that's so terribly different from anyone else? He struggles like the rest of us...he hasn't enough...of everything. How is that different from Pania Andreyevna? Because he wasn't fool enough to push a bloody train? Why did it need to be pushed anyway?

PANIA: You couldn't have done it.

INNA: But why should you? Is that post-Soviet freedom, is it? The train doesn't work, and there's not enough brown.

PANIA: There – she's solved the mystery of the ages. We can all go home to bed.

INNA: All right, laugh. But if Pishchik goes with him, I'm no longer working for you.

VOLKOV: It's out of her hands, dear – he's broken the law.

INNA: I don't care what he's done – that's what I'm prepared to do.

PANIA: And after that, what – your exceptional art? *(To VOLKOV.)* Perhaps she'll wait for him through prison.

INNA: Is he going to release him?

PANIA *(A beat.)*: To hell with both of you...I don't care what you do. *(As INNA shuffles past her.)* Hey, what do you think you're doing? I said I didn't care. You're not going to make me either. You can just put that back.

INNA has taken a brown loaf from a tray.

INNA: What if you were to release him in my care?

PANIA: She doesn't know what she's saying.

INNA *(Giving VOLKOV the brown loaf.)*: But you know that's not true, don't you?

PANIA: Congratulations.

VOLKOV *(To PANIA.)*: You've got to admit...he's not nearly as bad as some that are still roaming wild.

PANIA: You release him so they can play doll's house together. Doesn't that make you uplifted?

VOLKOV: Don't worry – I'll still keep my eye out for him.

INNA: I promise you – he'll be all right.

PANIA: They're going to 'complete each other's destinies' – how fulfilling can life ever be?

VOLKOV: Well, I'll tell you – if there's nothing else I can do for you...

PANIA: Don't let on that any of this happened under my roof. I'd never live it down.

VOLKOV (As he leaves.): I'm not even sure what time it is.

A pause.

PANIA (To INNA.): If you're serious, you'll get him out of here fast. Look at the damage he's caused.

INNA: He's got a cottage nearby? (As PANIA crosses the space out of view.) Don't worry, I'll come right back.

PANIA (Slightly off.): I mean it – I don't care what you do. You can go off to live in a cave, for all I care. I'm still looking for the third degree of sleep.

INNA is now alone with OSIP.

INNA (Bending over him.): Mr Osip...are you conscious?

OSIP (Suddenly very much alive.): So you've considered my proposal...and it's yes?

INNA: I can't marry you, my dear. It wouldn't be decent, like they said. I'm...I'm young enough to be your daughter. But I do want to thank you most sincerely, and to greet you with all of my heart. I never dreamed about anything like this.

OSIP: I'm very young, they tell me, in my heart.

INNA: Yes, in a most particular way – I can see it – you've no age at all. (Kisses him.)

OSIP: That means –

INNA: I know very well what it means, my dear.

OSIP: ...no! That I'm not going to die. Isn't that...!

INNA: Are you sure you can walk all right?

OSIP: Walk? Wings of steel, I have. I can just about fly.

INNA (Cheerful.): You'll have to wait for me then...I'm slow.

They leave the space supporting each other as the lights fade.

THE SWEETHEART ZONE

A Play

Performed as part of a second-year module by Drama students of the University of Exeter, under the direction of Martin Harvey, on 23 January 2007.

MISHA SHATKOVSKY	Nick Cosslet
NINA	Kate Kalvinos
ZHENIA	Katie Brayne
NADIA	Harri Dobby
LUDKA	Nikki Valvis
GRANNY	Lucy Holland
'LOLA'	Alice Beaumont
SHURA	Leah Peregrine-Lewis
YULIA	Ruth Ley
JACQUI	Chloe Nicholson
ENGLISH TANYA	Lucy Hill
POLYA	Emma Tomlinson
RAISA	Lucy Drewett
AMIRA	Kelly Ward
JADVIGA	Esther Finney
'EVA BRAUN'	Annabel Norbury
DR. ORLOVA	Helen Bryer
KOMANDIR	Catherine Downes
ASKA	Victoria Horn
VALODIA	Simon Cox

The women's zone of a labour camp on the Volga in post-Soviet Russia.

Character descriptions

MISHA SHATKOVSKY Career secret policeman, forties, with a family and a reasonably sized flat. Against stereotype, Misha is ordinary and honest.

NINA One of the zone's leaders by virtue of her personal history. In her late thirties. Father blinded in combat, so Nina looked after him until his death. Her crime was to lead a protest against punitive taxes on street merchants, incurring the hostility of local Duma member, a politician with dubious business interests.

ZHENIA Grade One (most severely) disabled, she was imprisoned probably for nothing more serious than alleged vagrancy. In and out of various homes for most of her 32 years.

NADIA Another of the zone's leaders. Alleged to have carried out a mercy killing, she probably did nothing more than watch helplessly as her daughter died of a miscarriage. In her mid-40s.

LUDKA Severely mentally challenged and imprisoned for it, she had a job painting railway sidings and such. Fellow workers on one job got drunk, fell asleep and died from the paint fumes. Ludka was blamed. In her forties. She has a strong sense of being beset by evil demons, everywhere.

GRANNY Zone matriarch, close to 60, she conceals a dark secret about why she is here.

'LOLA' Now 30, she married a teacher in her teens, and he made life miserable for her with his jealousy. She murdered him as a result.

SHURA Early thirties, vampish, the boss's favourite until a new woman came on the scene, then Shura went berserk.

YULIA Early thirties, in prison for a trifle. Wants to be popular.

JACQUI Late twenties. Street-wise by virtue of an unconventional lifestyle. Served short sentence for drugs, worked as a maid for a Mayfair prostitute.

ENGLISH TANYA Late twenties. First extended stay abroad. Works in a travel agency.

POLYA and RAISA Late teens, transfers from juvenile camp. Arrested for vagrancy, they have lived so far by various dubious means short of prostitution.

AMIRA Mid-30s. Jewish in a widely anti-semitic Russia, she faces immediate prejudice and plays up to it by currying favour with the prison authorities.

JADVIGA Early thirties. A Balt in post-Soviet Russia, she instantly arouses the antagonism of anyone aware of her origins. Probably imprisoned for letting her temporary residence permit lapse.

'EVA BRAUN' Early thirties. Relatively new prison warder, specially recruited for this assignment.

DR. ORLOVA Early forties. Her namesake was Soviet Russia's first mega film star, and Dr. Orlova benefits from this to the extent of inspiring maternal trust among the inmates. She deserves it, though her loyalty, in the end, is toward the authorities.

KOMANDIR Early forties. A Soviet-era 'aparatchik' with little patience for western-style humanism. These women, to her, are scum.

ASKA Late twenties. Imprisoned for a trifling offence, she has been put in solitary because it is known that she is the sister of a secret policeman who may be involved in counter-government activity.

VALODIA Mid-20s. New to the prison service, ex-military. Probably served in Chechnya.

The audience doubles as a group of official observers, presumably watching the prisoners from behind wire netting. A lone man, MISHA SHATKOVSKY, stands out. The women periodically address their remarks to him. A searchlight combs the compound. Then the prisoners are marched out in three groups of five. They are in blacks with white headscarves round their heads and grey identity triangles on their chests. The compound consists of the yard, a large work shed, the dormitory and 'infirmary'/psycho unit. Two of the groups are made up of seasoned inmates. The third, of new arrivals, is desultory. They huddle together in twos, with a lone inmate hovering round them. She is a Latvian named JADVIGA.

TANNOY: All right then, inmates. Nice and tidy and wide awake!

SHURA (Second group.): What the hell for?

NADIA (First group.): They don't want to torture us in our sleep.

YULIA (Second group.): Afraid we won't feel the full effect.

NINA (First group, shielding her eyes from the searchlight.): I don't like the way the sun's glaring at me.

LOLA (Separating herself from the first group; directly addressing the audience.): What the fuck do you think you're doing?

MISHA: We're only here to observe you. Try not to notice us.

GRANNY (First group, older.): You don't want your name taken, do you, my dear?

LOLA: What do you think we are, monkeys...at the fucking zoo? (*Making a face at MISHA.*) That's right. I'm talking to you.

YULIA: Don't wet yourself over it.

LOLA: Yeah? And what do you know about anything? (*To MISHA.*) Is she your girlfriend or something?

MISHA: Can't you stand friendly interest?

LOLA: From a sex maniac?

NINA (*Crossing toward the third group.*): Granny's right, though. If you start anything, they'll take you down.

MISHA: Take you down where? Come on, girls. I'm on your side.

LOLA: That's a laugh and three quarters! (*To NINA.*) D'you see them?

NINA: I see them all right – I'm not sightless, am I? (*To MISHA.*) Try not to take such obvious pleasure. We're just like everybody else, even with our clothes off.

SHURA: Maybe he finds us attractive...irresistible even.

LOLA: I'll give them all irresistible...rend the atmosphere thick with words they hope they've forgotten.

MISHA: We're not here to piss you off, I promise you.

YULIA: I heard them say he's a KGB spy.

NINA (*To the third group.*): So you girls have only just arrived.

TANNOY: Get back into line there.

LOLA: Why don't you come here and lick my arse!

NINA: At least you can turn off the searchlight – it's daybreak.

TANNOY: Go back to your own line, Petrova.

NINA: I'll stay right here with the rookies.

JADVIGA: We don't want troubles for you.

NINA: You're not Russian?

JADVIGA: None of us. From Latvia, me.

POLYA (*Whispering, to RAISA.*): What's a fucking Balt doing here?

NINA (*To POLYA and RAISA.*): You're Russian, aren't you? Sparrows from juve camp.

RAISA (*To POLYA.*): Don't tell her anything.

NINA: You're going to get awfully fed up...nobody else to talk to.

JADVIGA (*Of the remaining two.*): From USA.

NINA: Is that right, Americans?

JACQUI: English. (*To MISHA.*) Do you understand, mister? Sir? They locked us up here for no reason.

MISHA smiles vaguely.

TANYA: He thinks you're flirting with him. (*To MISHA.*) But we're not on the game, honest.

JACQUI: What makes you think he understands you any better?

TANYA (*Whispers.*): I don't give a flying (fart).

MISHA (*Whispers.*): I wish I could help you.

NINA (*Smiling, with gestures.*): My name...Nina.

JACQUI: Oh. Right. My name's Jacqui...and this is Tanya.

NINA: Tanya? You? But then you're Russian.

JACQUI: No, no, no, no...Tanya is English as well. We are English.

TANYA: I'm going to be mental, at this rate.

NINA: He is...KGB. You know, secret policeman?

TANYA: Oh, God. That's all we need.

TANNOY: All right, you toe-suckers. Back into line.

SHURA: Where do you think we are?

LOLA: You tell us, please, what we're doing here.

AMIRA: I can tell you...I just heard all about it.

AMIRA'S entrance causes a small stir. No one speaks for a moment. POLYA has her eyes fixed on ZHENIA, a disabled woman in the first group. Her mate, NADIA, becomes gradually upset.

SHURA: All right, nark, tell us.

AMIRA: I keep telling you, I'm not a nark. I'm just back from 'psycho', aren't I?

YULIA: So you keep telling us. *(To her group.)* Something very dodgy about a person that has to announce her good intentions all the time. Don't you agree with me, ladies?

General hubbub.

AMIRA: ...and something even worse about a shit-stirrer.

SHURA: I couldn't agree more. You're that as well...which makes you even –

General hubbub.

GRANNY *(To AMIRA.)*: Just tell us your news, lovie. Are they going to reduce our rations again?

AMIRA: They've appointed a new 'executive officer' to oversee us... 'Exec'...get it?

NINA *(To JADVIGA and the others.)*: A 'zek' is the slang term for 'inmate'.

YULIA: Are you trying to say he's an ex-convict? *(General: 'Oh, charming...' 'That means he'll be even worse.')*

AMIRA: I'm trying to say it's a woman...what you asked for, after all.

LOLA *(To the audience.)*: Did you lot have anything to do with it?

AMIRA: Aren't you always sending protest letters to Moscow? Talk about shit-stirrers. *(To MISHA.)* She's the one that brought you here, right?

MISHA: We're not here on anyone's say-so. But can't you tell me, please. What did she mean by 'psycho'?

SHURA *(To AMIRA.)*: We remember how you didn't sign.

MISHA: What did they do to you there?

AMIRA *(To MISHA.)*: I can't talk to you. *(To NINA.)* I'm telling you now how they've gone and answered you. I just heard about it.

YULIA: You didn't catch sight of her, did you?

AMIRA: No, but I heard her referred to as a terror, nicknamed Eva Braun, to prove it.

SHURA *(Derisively.)*: Eva Braun!

AMIRA *(Pointing.)*: And there she is!

'EVA BRAUN' appears above, imperious, like a Soviet commissar.

EVA BRAUN: You were told to get into line...like you do every morning. Don't for a second imagine my regime's going to be any different, except, very possibly, harder.

General grumbling.

AMIRA: See what I mean?

EVA BRAUN: Well, isn't this just what you asked for – a woman exec?

YULIA: Why don't you meet us, then, on our level, face-to-face?

LOLA: And are you responsible for that lot out there? Is he also part of your 'regime'?

EVA BRAUN *(Descending.)*: You'll find it easier to pretend they're not there.

NADIA: What, like the bugging devices planted by our beds?

GENERAL: 'Don't say a word'; 'Can't even talk out here now' etc.

EVA BRAUN: Well, you could try confiding your troubles to him.

NADIA: One Day in the Life of Masha Denisova.

JACQUI *(Nudging TANYA.)*: I think they're talking about those people out there.

TANYA: Tourists at Auschwitz.

EVA BRAUN: Well! People are very interested. Aren't you meant to be the world-famous 'sweetheart zone'? You'll probably be asked for your autographs.

LUDKA *(First group, addressing audience.)*: Can you really help us? What's your reason for being here? Someone cast a spell...didn't they?

NADIA: It's an obvious trap. Can't you see? That's the face of a government thug.

EVA BRAUN: All right, then, keep stum. You'll be making my job that much easier.

LOLA: I think she's a regular cream puff. *(To EVA BRAUN.)* That right? Your name's loaded with irony, isn't it?

YULIA: What, like you're loaded with horse shit?

NADIA: What are you getting on Lola's case for?

NINA: Of course, we're sweet.

GRANNY: How else could we look after each other?

NADIA: Well said, Granny dear.

EVA BRAUN: Then it's obvious we're a match. My name... *(Jeers.)* For those who don't know it, my name is Volkova...Marina?

LOLA *(Derisively.)*: Say that again, please. Vulcan?

General laughter.

EVA BRAUN: I heard your last chief was called Lionheart.

LOLA: Lionheart?

SHURA *(Laughter.)*: And Littlebrain!

YULIA: Liverlips!

EVA BRAUN: And yet you complained about my predecessor! *(Noise.)* Why else do you think I'm here?

LOLA: She'll tell us next she's our union rep!

EVA BRAUN: Okay, we've had our friendly joke. *(Noise.)* The men's camp is only over that wall.

LOLA *(To MISHA.)*: Is that where you're from?

YULIA: Maybe they're really lovers. *(To MISHA.)* That right, lover? *(Makes a lascivious gesture toward him.)*

MISHA: I'm really trying to help you. *(Makes a farting noise.)*

EVA BRAUN: I'll send you there one at a time if we don't get some order here in the next twenty seconds! *(Points gun. Hush.)* That's more like it. I'll be calling the roll here, and with each name your individual task for the morning.

NADIA: What do you mean, task?

SHURA: We all know what we do here.

NINA: All except the rookies.

SHURA: They'll find out.

EVA BRAUN: That's why we're having a general review. Besides, I mean to try something new my first day. You're in favour of that, aren't you?

NINA: Don't make out you're giving us options.

GENERAL: 'You tell her, Ninochka.'

NINA: We sew gloves and very little else...sometimes mailbags.

LOLA: The occasional woollen knicker, eh, Granny?

EVA BRAUN: You're still going to do that, don't worry. But this compound is more like a pig pen, come on.

SHURA: It's more like a prison, what do you want?

EVA BRAUN: A garden of tulips! *(General hooting.)* Isn't that just what you asked for...what you want? *(Above the din.)* What's the point of having a woman in charge?

LOLA: To practise homosex without getting caught!

NINA: Hang on, ladies! *(To EVA BRAUN.)* Are you serious, an actual garden?

YULIA: To grow carrots and beetroot and spuds?

EVA BRAUN: Oh, no, I said flowers – tulips, or daffs, if you want.

YULIA: What's the point of that? You can't eat them.

SHURA: What do you bet?

LOLA (To the audience.): I bet it's on account of you lot.

SHURA: I'll swallow anything that doesn't taste of slurry. Even tulip bulbs.

EVA BRAUN: You lot are just wasting time.

SHURA: You eat sunflower seeds, don't you? Russian chocolates?

YULIA: You don't have any, do you?

EVA BRAUN: I have the rota all worked out.

NADIA: Rota? I thought she said 'roll'.

SHURA (To EVA BRAUN.): You don't have to worry, dear. There's no place for us to escape to.

LOLA: I think we ought to discuss this first...maybe put it to a voice vote.

EVA BRAUN: Belova, north garden.

NADIA: 'Belova, north garden'...what does that mean?

EVA BRAUN (Pointing.): Over there.

NINA (Whispering, to LOLA.): I don't think we're given a choice.

EVA BRAUN: Budina, north garden...Zhukova, north garden...Larina, north... You'd better hurry.

NADIA, POLYA, AMIRA and SHURA have separated from their respective groups but do not form a group of their own.

NADIA: What is this, Get-Acquainted Day?

SHURA: Let's suppose for a moment I don't want her (AMIRA) near me.

POLYA: Raisa and I are the new ones. Are you separating us just for spite?

NINA: I'll go with you, whatever happens.

POLYA: Well, thanks, but I'd just as soon...

NADIA: Wait a minute. Look. We're already in groups. Why don't we just take the north side here, and then they can –

EVA BRAUN: Not all of you have been allocated gardening duties.

General hum.

NADIA: I don't understand. I thought this was gardening detail.

EVA BRAUN: Some of you will have to continue with sewing. The quota, I understand, is 50 pair per person per day.

LOLA: She probably wants them to make up the shortfall. (To EVA BRAUN.) Now I see how you came by your nickname.

NINA: All right, how many and who, exactly?

JACQUI: I haven't a clue what's going on.

TANYA: I think she's checking names.

JACQUI: Then maybe they've missed us.

JADVIGA: She give us all our job.

JACQUI: You speak English!

JADVIGA: Little only.

EVA BRAUN: Everybody's on gardening duty except...

LOLA: ...except...?

JADVIGA (Whispering.): They ask for us dig.

JACQUI: Dig? Dig what?

TANYA: Our own graves, it looks like.

EVA BRAUN: ...Fedina and Kuzina.

GENERAL: 'What!' 'Why only two?' etc.

EVA BRAUN: You two will carry on with the sewing. *(Consulting her paper.)* Mironova, south garden....

YULIA: There's not going to be enough garden.

NADIA: I think there's been some mistake.

LOLA: There's no mistake, sweetheart. They planned it this way.

SHURA: Yeah...why only two?

NADIA: You've chosen the two who never do sewing. Why?

EVA BRAUN: Exactly. It's time they started.

LOLA: I told you.

POLYA *(To RAISA, though her eyes have been on ZHENIA.)*: I was afraid they'd put her with us.

NADIA: Back me up, will you, Nina. *(To EVA BRAUN.)* But they can't sew. Zhen, in particular. By rights, she shouldn't be here.

EVA BRAUN: Correct me if I'm mistaken. She is here...and this is a labour camp, not a Black Sea resort?

NADIA: But...just look at her.

EVA BRAUN: I can't take my eyes off her – so what?

NINA: She's crippled, Chief.

NADIA: Any fool can see that.

NINA: She's never gone near a machine.

EVA BRAUN: What is she then, the camp mascot?

ZHENIA: Don't make excuses for me, girls. *(To EVA.)* I can do the work.

EVA BRAUN: You hear that? She's itching to start.

NADIA: All right, let me go in her place. She'll dig a wonderful garden for you. That's more or less what she does. She's the zone's Cinderella. That's –

EVA BRAUN: I know what that is. Every camp has one.

NADIA: Well, she's ours.

NINA: And Ludka doesn't work a machine either – she's –

EVA BRAUN: Cinder's assistant, I suppose.

NINA: Ludka, dear. This is the new chief's first day on the job. She'd be grateful if you could give her your name.

LUDKA: Last night I assumed the form of the Grand Duchess Anastasya. (*Looking at MISHA.*) Rudolpho asked me to the ball. I don't like to torment a heart.

NADIA: Satisfied? It's for real, you know.

MISHA: I don't know anything about it.

EVA BRAUN: Don't encourage them then. They said you're just here to observe.

NINA: She'd be likely to sew all the gloves without fingers. That's the point.

EVA BRAUN: You're saying she belongs in the psycho ward.

NINA: All we're saying, in all honesty –

EVA BRAUN: That's the only other place for either of them. Now you'll find the spades and other gardening implements...

General din.

EVA BRAUN (*Voice raised.*): This isn't a matter for general debate.

LOLA (*To the audience.*): What do you think? Is this a proper way to run a prison? It's not true there are no political prisoners any more. Tell the media, will you? We're all political.

JACQUI (*To JADVIGA.*): Can you get someone to get in touch with our Embassy?

JADVIGA (*With gestures.*): Cannot hear you.

JACQUI: The British Embassy. We're the victims of false arrest. It's some scuzz-ball pimp that's the real culprit!

TANYA: That's going to make them drop everything.

EVA BRAUN: Shut the fuck up, the whole fucking lot of you! *(Beat.)* Where's that Balt? *(Spotting JADVIGA.)* You.

JADVIGA: I'm from Riga, Madame. Jadviga Glazevsky.

EVA BRAUN: Thrilled to bits that you told me that, sweetheart. *(To the group.)* You all see her? She's the new Cinderella. Come with me.

JADVIGA: But I have to translate....tell them

They go off and there is a momentary hush.

NADIA *(Breaking the silence.)*: 'Eva Braun' was far too demure, if you ask me. She's more like the Beast of Belsen – what's her name? Ilse...Ilse Krupp.

YULIA: Don't tempt fate.

POLYA: Where's she taken her, the psycho ward? What's that?

YULIA: Punishment wing...they keep you on half rations...chained to the wall.

AMIRA *(Going from group to group.)*: She really belongs in the sick bay...on her way to the cemetery. She's the last one we want as our Cinderella. No doubt that's the idea...to kill us off painfully...one or two at a time.

NINA *(Explaining to POLYA and RAISA.)*: She's the one we elect to test things out for us.

AMIRA: Yes, that's it – fetch and carry and cook and clean. Haven't you noticed the sores on her arms and forehead? I got close enough.

NINA: She's trying to say she's syphilitic, like every other foreigner who finds her way in here. *(To AMIRA.)* That's right, isn't it?

AMIRA: Not just syphilis, my dears...speed.

NINA: One day you'll go too far.

AMIRA: Threaten me all you like. I saw her lesions.

YULIA: Then maybe you've got it.

JACQUI *(To TANYA.)*: Do you have a clue what they're talking about?

TANYA: They took her off, for some reason.

AMIRA: Sick. She has... *(Gestures.)* ...you know?

JACQUI: I don't like the sound of that. You suppose she means Aids?

TANYA: Why should that matter to you?

JACQUI: I'm not HIV.

TANYA: We both are, thanks to your friends.

JACQUI: Then you've nothing to worry about either.

MISHA: That is not what the guard said.

JACQUI: You speak English!

TANYA: Can you get us out of here? They said you're...

MISHA: They are fools only. I will can translate. The guards asks her to carry. *(Of AMIRA.)* This one...make scandal. Must be what they call parrot.

JACQUI: We had them in England.

TANYA: That's what you were, eh?

MISHA: Possible we help each other.

A solitary cell in the psycho ward. ASKA is trying to carry the slop bucket across the space to the back, where she will be permitted to deposit the waste. But the bucket is heavy and she falters. There is the sound of clanking keys. ASKA cowers. VALODIA comes on.

VALODIA: Jesus Christ! *(Crosses to her. Helps her to her feet.)* You didn't try to lift that yourself, did you. That's a two-zek job.

ASKA: And I'm in solitary.

VALODIA: Yeah, I know, but the least they could do is help you with it...if they want to keep you alive.

ASKA: Maybe that's it. Maybe they just want me dead.

VALODIA: No, they want you alive, take my word for it.

ASKA: Why should I? Why the fuck – ?

VALODIA: 'cause I wouldn't be here otherwise. (*Helps her sit down on a bench.*) Are you all right now? And don't worry no more about the bucket. I'll empty it now and tell them they've got to help you from now on. You're not on hunger strike, are you? That's just stupid. It's so cold in here, you risk not being able to have babies anyway. If you starve yourself as well...

ASKA: I'm not on strike.

VALODIA: Yeah, well, that's a good thing. For you, I mean. They couldn't give a...a Chechen's balls. They'd just take this long plastic tube through your nose...and you wouldn't be able to breathe...

ASKA breaks down.

No, it's all right. You say you're not on strike, and you eat regular. Not a banquet, I know...

ASKA (*Wailing.*): I don't know why I'm here!

VALODIA: Yeah, well, I know. You're here for the same reason I'm here. To find out exactly what it is you...Don't you really know, honest? Jeez, that's going to land me right in the... (*Pointing to the contents of the bucket.*) in here. (*A beat.*) They couldn't have made a mistake.

ASKA: Oh, yes, I'm sure that's what they've done. It's all a mistake. It has to be. I've done nothing the other girls haven't done. In fact they've done even worse. Murder, one or two of them did.

VALODIA: Believe me, you're not like the others. By their lights at least.

ASKA: But just tell me. What have I done? I took a handbag. That's what I was accused of anyway. And then when I was interviewed by the police, I wouldn't pay over a bribe.

VALODIA: That's just your cover story.

ASKA: It's what happened.

VALODIA: They think there has to be more.

ASKA: But can't you tell me...what they think it is.

VALODIA (*A beat.*): All right. I'm going to lay it on the line. They don't think you're just like the others...the minnows. Even the nymphet that bumped off her old man. The ones you hear three times a week over Prison Radio, including the pissheads. 'I drank to get over my sad love affair...and then I stole in order to drink...and then my lover took over my flat, with his family.' God in heaven, you're not one of those. Are you?

ASKA: I didn't even take the bag.

VALODIA: I believe you. So do they. About the bag anyway. But what I don't get – and what you're going to help me with – is why they should call you 'political'.

ASKA: But I'm not. I swear to you...cold sober. What's 'political' anyway?

VALODIA: They're convinced you can tell me.

ASKA: And who are you? You're not another bent policeman, are you? You offered to help me...you said someone would help me...with the bucket. You remember? There's no such thing as political any more. You know that.

VALODIA: And you never once carried a message for someone?

ASKA: I mean...look at me. I'm shitting myself!

VALODIA: Not even for a member of your family?

Scene shift.

NADIA (*Dovetailing.*): What about it, ladies? Are we going to let Zhenia do the sewing on her own? (*To the audience.*) Any doubt in your mind that it was deliberate? I'm telling you. She has no business being here. It's not like she committed a crime, except being born like she is.

YULIA: You want us to withdraw our labour...maybe even a hunger strike. And for what, exactly?

NADIA: What do you mean, for what? For Zhenia!

POLYA: The last thing I want is a hunger strike.

SHURA: That's right. I want to know when we're going to eat.

YULIA: It's normally right after roll-call.

SHURA: And it's normally no more than gruel.

RAISA: It's not so much hungry as thirsty...my God!

SHURA: Don't tell me. They gave you fish when they met you off the Moscow train and drove you here.

YULIA: A special sort of herring – added salt to make you crazy with thirst.

RAISA: Have you got anything...?

YULIA: ...and then force you to drink your own piss. *(Starting to move.)* I keep my jar right next to Shura's.

RAISA: Keep your jar...of your own urine?

YULIA: That way you never run short.

RAISA: No, don't...show me.

YULIA: I was going to offer you some.

General laughter.

POLYA: Can't you tell when your leg's being pulled?

NINA: I don't know. The way the tea's brewed, it does often taste like a form of waste. *(Passes her a mug of tea.)* This was fresh this morning.

RAISA: What is it?

NINA: Bless us and keep us...tea.

RAISA: What else is in it?

NINA: I think Granny added a strawberry leaf for flavour.

RAISA: Th-that's all right.

NINA: I know it's all right...it's freshly brewed tea!

POLYA: She's never going to believe you.

NINA: She'll die of thirst then. *(She downs the tea in one.)* Care to smell my breath?

LOLA: Any more where that came from? I mean tea.

The women begin to move toward the area where the first group stood. ZHENIA sets about serving them.

NADIA: What are we going to do about Zhenia?

ZHENIA: And Ludka, too, don't forget.

NADIA: Why don't we take it in turns to do her shift?

ZHENIA: You can't ask them to do that.

NADIA: You keep out of it. Hang on. Ladies? If I go with her to sew the first ten...who's going second? You'll help us, won't you, Neen?

NINA: If that's what we decide, sure.

NADIA: Who's got a better idea?

ZHENIA: I can do what I can by myself. I'm not helpless.

NADIA: Sure, you are. She's setting you up, like Lola said.

LOLA: Lola said what? Who's quoting my words in vain?

NADIA (To MISHA.): You're authorized to report this, right? It's deliberate provocation. You can tell them so.

MISHA: I can tell them anything you like, if only you'll tell me. Can you tell me about the punishments?

LOLA: In your dreams, nark.

NINA: Whether it was or it wasn't provocation, what's helping Zhenia going to achieve?

NADIA: Are you serious? I can't believe you said that, Nina.

NINA: I mean we can refuse altogether. (To POLYA.) What? (POLYA whispers something.) And I don't think we should ask the new girls, anyway.

NADIA: All right, but there's nearly a dozen of us.

POLYA: I meant she makes me nervous.

RAISA: She's afraid to be around people like her.

NADIA: People like who?

RAISA: Ask her about it. I'm going to get some of that... *(Pushes past the women near her to the area where tea is being served.)*

NADIA *(To NINA.)*: Did you hear that? *(To POLYA.)* Someone just might take a sudden and violent dislike to you.

GRANNY: I think I have an answer for what we might do.

AMIRA *(To LOLA.)*: That Balt has been gone an awfully long time.

LOLA: Why don't you ring her up?

AMIRA: I tell you they've taken her...

GRANNY *(Overlapping.)*: We resume our practice of knitting woollens, those of us that feel the cold.

YULIA: You're talking about all of us.

NADIA: That's what I said – we take it in turns.

GRANNY: No, no. With this, none of us go anywhere near the machines.

NADIA: Including Zhenia.

GRANNY: Especially Zhenia. *(To ZHENIA.)* We must do what we can to protect you, my dear.

ZHENIA: I can't let you take the risk, Granny. Ludka and I'll just have to do what we can. We'll cope, eh, Lud?

LUDKA: Anyone with black eyes has the Devil himself for a near relation. *(To MISHA.)* Not a brother-in-law ten times removed. I mean blood close. *(She whimpers.)*

MISHA: What's the matter with her? *(To LUDKA.)* Were you beaten?

NINA *(Crossing to comfort her.)*: You frightened her, what do you think? *(To LUDKA.)* Just look into our eyes, Lud. They're only blue.

LOLA: I'll give anybody five buckshee to spit in his eye.

NINA: All right, Lo.

LOLA: You'd do it for big American bucks, wouldn't you, Lud?

NINA: I said, all right.

LUDKA *(Tearfully.)*: Why were you reading my letters?

MISHA: She's crazy. I'm not here to hurt anyone.

NINA: And just how does that excuse you? You're a government nark.

MISHA: Maybe I'm more of a friend than you think. But I just asked what's wrong with her.

LOLA: She's bewitched.

GRANNY: Would somebody pass me that bag from over there? Don't you do it, Zhenia. *(To LOLA.)* You're full of beans this morning, Larissa Osipovna.

LOLA: I didn't know you knew my real name.

GRANNY: Right over there behind the sluice buckets.

LOLA *(Crossing to the buckets.)*: Did you all hear that? Larissa, not a tramp.

NINA *(To RAISA.)*: We called her Lolita when she told us she married a teacher when young. *(To LOLA.)* We called you that out of affection.

LOLA: You were jealous as hell.

NINA: Well, that in itself is a tribute.

LOLA *(Of the bag's contents.)*: What the hell is this!

GRANNY: Bring it here and I'll show you.

LOLA: What did you do, rob a warehouse? *(General reaction.)* Did you know this was here, girls? Reams of it! Finest cotton! How in the world did you ever get...! *(Showing NINA.)* It's the real thing, eh, Nina?

NINA: I'm sure it is.

The women gravitate toward that area.

SHURA: Who did you find to bribe?

GRANNY *(Conscious of MISHA.)*: Don't show it to everybody.

NINA: This looks like surgical...It's from the infirmary!

GRANNY *(To MISHA.)*: They'd sell us anything for the right price.

LOLA collects the bits the women are inspecting and takes the bag over to GRANNY. A number of them follow her.

SHURA: I'll bet most of those were taken off corpses.

NINA: They're not going to be missed then.

GRANNY: Most of it, really, was confiscated.

SHURA: You mean it's our own stuff.

GENERAL: 'I had a silk shimmy they were pleased to take off me'/ 'I had some silk smalls'... etc.

NINA: How did you manage to buy it all back? With what?

GRANNY: You want me to tell you my secrets? *(As she sorts through the bits.)* I think someone should tell our foreign guests about the zone's underwear policy.

AMIRA *(With gestures.)*: You must...you know...strip!

TANYA: Fuck off.

JACQUI: Why? Is it some lesbian ritual?

MISHA: It's a joke, huh?

GRANNY: No, no, no, we don't ask you. But first step punishment...strip to your bras and –

JACQUI: – knickers, I got you. Punishment for what?

GRANNY: Anything they want. Zhenia, the cripple, was ordered to work on machines. If she does not, she will need to strip and stand out in the cold.

JACQUI: Jesus, for how long?

MISHA: Maybe when she will dead.

AMIRA: That's right.

GRANNY *(In translation.)*: But you did not tell them about their culottes. If you have anythings like French underwears, they will either be stolen or you will die of the cold.

TANYA *(To JACQUI.)*: I could kill you right now, myself...save them the trouble.

JACQUI: Oh, grow up. These ladies are coping, aren't they? And I made it through two years in Holloway.

TANYA: Jailbirds!

JACQUI: No, it's like travelling in India. The quickest way to get sick as a budgerigar is to order their English cuisine everywhere you go. If you eat what the natives eat –

TANYA: You can spare me your eastern philosophy. *(To MISHA.)* But you're an official of some kind, aren't you? You've got to speak up for us.

MISHA: No, no, I am no things. If they catched me speak with you even –

JACQUI: You must have contacts at our embassy...You've probably been posted to London in your time?

TANYA *(Frustrated.)*: Anybody out there been raped and speaks English?

JACQUI: Oh, eff off!

MISHA: I do not understand. You want to know about –

JACQUI: She's having a laugh. That's what journalists ask when they arrive in a foreign city. She must have read that somewhere.

MISHA: English journalists.

JACQUI: Of course. It's a joke, really.

MISHA: Different cultures. First question in Russia is who you must pay.

TANYA: I'm not arsed. *(To MISHA.)* What'll you take to get us out of here? How much?

MISHA: I coulds do little for you, really.

TANYA *(To AMIRA.)*: All right...who do you know?

JACQUI *(As though AMIRA is fluent.)*: You see, Tanya's pissed off 'cause she was arrested for being a prostitute. But...I mean she's not...We were both staying at this tourist hotel.

TANYA: Can't you see you're wasting your –

MISHA: Intourist? They arrested you there?

JACQUI: I guess that's where it was. And it was a mistake, of course. I mean...it's ridiculous.

TANYA: Will you shut the...up? (To audience.) Don't pay any attention.

JACQUI: But I've worked for a prostitute back in London...in Soho, although she moved up market to somewhere in Mayfair.

TANYA: Great. They'll think you're my lesbian pimp.

JACQUI. Oh, no! I was Gillian's maid. Gillian, the woman I worked for. And I clean up for her... answer the door to clients. It was all very...nice really. I know that must be hard to imagine.

MISHA: I do not think any imagine it.

JACQUI: Well, I know. That's what I'm –

MISHA: I do not know that I image it. You were in prison for cleaning house?

JACQUI: That was something else entirely.

TANYA: ...for being a druggie.

JACQUI: For having a partner who was a druggie. He dealt drugs, that was the point.

TANYA: The point is, he left you holding the stash...and she's right. Nobody knows what you're talking about or could give a fuck.

JACQUI: I don't care. I'm as narked off about it as you are, and I needed to tell somebody. So. Thanks for listening.

TANYA: They had no choice.

JACQUI: Yes, they did. Oh, yes. I almost forgot. I'm more used to this than she is. That was my real –

TANYA (Dovetailing.): If there's anybody out there who knows any English...

JACQUI: Being raped is optional, I guess.

Overlapping this, the other inmates are seen taking an interest in GRANNY'S project, so AMIRA makes her way over there.

SHURA: Do you know what? This isn't too bad. As ideas go.

GRANNY: It'll save many a kidney. *(To POLYA and RAISA.)* That's what I can't understand about young girls. You want to risk your lives every time you go out – half naked, for fashion.

POLYA: You got me wrong, grandma. I'm not stripping on no one's account.

RAISA: That's true. The bathhouse might be another town, for all the notice she takes. *(Drains her mug.)* Great pee, by the way. That strawberry leaf is like sugar.

POLYA: Why don't I give you real pee? You're almost stupid enough to drink it.

NINA *(Suddenly bursting out laughing.)*: I remember once riding in a bus, this drunk got up and all the way down the aisle he kept muttering, 'Right side, idiots; left side, whores.' And finally, when he got within two seats of me, the woman stood up and announced: 'You're quite wrong. I am not what you called me. I never had a lover in my life!' To which he replied, calm as Christmas, 'In that case, you sit over there!' *(Laughs.)*

AMIRA: And which side of the aisle were you?

SHURA *(Overlapping.)*: How is it you never gave these to us before?

YULIA: Before what? It's been thirty degrees for the last umpteen weeks. You want to have fried kidneys?

NADIA: This would do for you, Ludka darling. *(Holds out her hand.)* Come sit by me. That's right. Now what we want you to do is take hold of the stitching in each piece of cloth and undo it, so that we then have many more pieces of cloth.

YULIA: That brings up an interesting problem, though, doesn't it?

NADIA: What do you mean?

YULIA: Which side of the bus would Lud have been on?

SHURA: She'd have had to stand in the middle!

POLYA *(Mocking.)*: And what did you have for your breakfast?

RAISA *(Giggles.)*: Fried kidneys and piss!

NADIA: You see that? They're only encouraged.

YULIA: Oh, for God's sake.

SHURA: No, no. You're quite right. Sorry, Nadia. I'm sorry, Lud. Seriously. Here, look. I'll get you started. Come on.

NADIA: Just leave well enough alone.

NINA: How can you wonder they treat her as strange when you protect her the whole time?

NADIA: Is that what you really think?

GRANNY: She thinks everyone is the devil.

SHURA: You trust us, don't you, Ludka? My eyes are azure blue...and I haven't got a tail.

NADIA: Shu-ra.

SHURA (Showing her the material.): You take hold of it like this...and if we were doing it professionally, we'd have scissors, of course. But that could be classed as a weapon.

GRANNY: You want this? (Holds out a small implement.)

SHURA: You must be a sorceress – yes! It's tiny but...this is exactly what it was made for.

POLYA: Got any more?

SHURA: It's Luda's job.

LUDKA: If it's mine, then let me have it.

SHURA: Certainly, my dear.

NADIA: She's not going to hurt herself, is she?

SHURA: She can't even hurt the stitch. (To LUDKA.) Silly Nadia.

LUDKA: Let me...have it! (She seizes hold of the material and tries to rip it apart with her hands, merely growing in frustration.)

NADIA: What are you forcing on her?

SHURA: You heard what your friends said, didn't you? Butt out of it. Liuda's just fine.

YULIA: Can you remember the paint work you did, Lud?

LUDKA (Continuing to struggle with the material.): I painted sidings.

YULIA: I know you did. You painted the football stadium, too.

LUDKA: Not the stadium...are you crazy? (Laughs.) I painted the seats.

YULIA: I beg your pardon, my dear.

SHURA: And then they asked you to paint the changing rooms, didn't they.

LUDKA: Don't remember.

SHURA: I think it's important that you try to, my lovely. Can you repeat after me? 'I...was...raped.'

NADIA: All right, get out of it...both of you.

SHURA: That's what happened, though, isn't it?

NADIA: Nina, help me with these maniacs, for God's sake. Have Zhenia prepare her some breakfast.

NINA (Arm round LUDKA.): Sure, but we can't watch over them every second. (To SHURA.) What did you do anyway?

SHURA: I was helping her with the stitching. Nadia's the one that said she should try.

NADIA: I'm not the one that upset her.

SHURA: Who said she's upset?

NADIA: 'Repeat after me!'

LUDKA: I remember being locked in a room in the cellar of...what was it?

YULIA: Stadium.

LUDKA: That's right. You asked me about that, didn't you? I was there with two men, and they told us to paint the whole room. But the room went dark, and the men fell asleep and the paint smelled just terrible. I climbed out through a window. And next day they told me the men didn't wake up.

NINA (To NADIA.): Is that what actually happened?

NADIA: I don't know.

NINA: Where did the rape come in?

SHURA: She must have been handled at some point.

NINA: Listen to me, Lud, very carefully. Okay? Did those men ever touch you?

LUDKA (*Angry and laughing.*): I told you – they went to sleep!

Perhaps a collective sigh.

YULIA: Did any man ever touch you?

NINA: No, I'm sorry. That's too much for her before breakfast.

ZHENIA (*Partially in view.*): I've been waiting since you asked me...how long is it now?

AMIRA: We were told not to eat until Speedy came back with the tools.

They ignore her, but only SHURA and YULIA follow LUDKA into the dining tent.

RAISA: Aren't you eating?

POLYA: What do you think?

NADIA: Both of you don't mind starving to death. Very interesting.

POLYA: That one's plain loco...and the crip makes me cringe.

NADIA: I warned you about that already.

POLYA: I just want to know where I am. They told me prison, but now I'm not sure. And what are you all doing humouring them? Is that your punishment? The place I was at before, they'd have left it to us to get rid of the likes of her.

GRANNY: And where was that, my dear?

POLYA: Does it matter? That's another thing. We were always told not to reveal why we were inside. It wasn't the done thing to ask.

NADIA: And why was that, do you think – it was unspeakably bad?

NINA: Our pasts are what draw us together. They inspire us.

GRANNY: We confess our sins. Isn't that right, Polya?

LOLA has been helping GRANNY sort through the old clothing. She addresses GRANNY but intends the other women to overhear.

LOLA: Sure, I'll bite. I'm not ashamed of killing my husband. *(To the audience.)* You got that, folks? And I was unfairly arrested for it, too.

GRANNY: He was well connected.

LOLA: He was a positive shit...I mean positively, he was –

SHURA: He caught you cheating on him, admit it.

LOLA: He saw me sharing my lunch on the bench with a schoolmate! We were 16 years old. You want to know what peeping is? Let me tell you. Boris would even hide out in the bushes.

NINA: Waiting to catch you making love?

LOLA: Watching...what...I did...in class.

SHURA: With your schoolmate...

LOLA: With the textbook! Lenin's additions to dialectical materialism, and there is my devoted spouse slobbering away like a diseased dog. Homeless, even. They're going to round him up, gas him and flog his fur for carpets.

SHURA: Except that you got there first.

LOLA: I smothered him with a cushion, yes. One of mother's finest heirlooms. Would you like me to give you the context, Inspector? He locked me out of the kitchen. Clever, eh? The noted professor who's so distinguished, he won't even allow his toy wife to have lunch...or breakfast or dinner...or anything at all. 'This is my food', he calmly announces one day before lunchtime. 'If you're hungry, fine, go earn your own.' And the law backed him up in this. Support a nymphet? She deserves to starve. Of course, I killed him. He could have been eaten to death.

GRANNY *(To ZHENIA.)*: Fetch her some porridge, love.

LOLA: No, I don't mean I'm hungry now.

GRANNY: Of course, you're hungry. Every one of us is, even poor Liuda Antipova...transformed into phantoms of our real selves.

ZHENIA has gone toward the dining area.

LOLA: That's really what happened to me.

NINA: And I think that's saying too much for Ludka.

GRANNY: And when we talk of personal histories, of course, yours is the one we all look to.

NINA: I'll help with the sewing, Granny, gladly. But if you don't mind...

GRANNY: She had a clothing stall in the local street market –

NINA: I really wish you wouldn't.

GRANNY: Better tell it yourself then, quick. The mayor wanted you out...

NINA: He wanted to shut us down, yes. My mother's protest was much more heroic.

GRANNY: But yours brought them out in the streets. 'People's enemy' was invoked in your honour.

NINA: It's true that we're all political prisoners.

GRANNY: Some more than others, my dear.

NINA: They raised the licensing tax...three times more than I made. They wanted us 'off the street'. (Tearfully.) Poor Galusik was killed for her efforts. I was merely...chased out of town. (Changing the subject quickly.) My mother was nearly arrested for talking to a neighbour in front of the Orthodox Church. They let her go when she told them my father fought at Stalingrad. He did fight at Stalingrad. He was blinded there. Had his fingers blown off as well.

AMIRA: And I tell you again and again I was arrested after the bastard I married threw my son into the fire. I called the police on him, so they arrested me.

NADIA: Have you no particle of shame? These women have risked their lives many times, and you mock them.

AMIRA: I'm a Christian! Like she is.

NADIA: And tell us next how you took Calvary's burden on your back...up the steps to Gethsemane.

AMIRA: Fine. You tell me how I come to be here.

SHURA: We all think you're a nark.

NADIA: I don't know. You probably kicked a halfwit to death.

AMIRA: But they're doing away with such people...so they'd thank me.

NADIA: Or maybe it was a policeman.

AMIRA: Well, then you should.

NADIA: I don't know. All any of us knows is...you're no hero.

GRANNY (*After a moment.*): Most of you must think I bribed someone a pretty penny for these fineries...the same as I bribed the city officials when I made and sold my moonshine for an unheard of profit. And you could have carried on with the town's blessing, Nina, if only you'd given the right person the right price.

NINA: I had nothing to give.

GRANNY: There's always something that someone wants badly enough.

NINA: It's true. I have a beautiful, talented niece that the mayor saw. She sang in the choir of the Baptist Church, and he asked if she'd sing at a friend's wedding. I wouldn't let her. She was the age Lola was when she married, and the mayor was scarcely proposing. So. I said she couldn't and paid for my niece's salvation with my own. No doubt Lola would say it was worth it.

GRANNY: But I paid with actual money, didn't I? The same as I did for these clothes. How is it that I, too, am in here with Lola and Nina and the rest of you sinners?

NINA: Does it matter?

NADIA: You were double-crossed.

GRANNY: It might matter, yes, to our sisters that think secrets are better kept secret. (*Beat.*) Our neighbour Petrovich was the best DIY specialist in our area. Larger. His renown was county wide. Friends would ask him to lay a forecourt and he'd do it himself, single-handed, within a day. And all I needed him for was a fence...repair job. Not even a new fence...which he could have erected, no problem, in almost the same amount of time. Why belittle a man for doing precisely what you ask...and for free. He didn't want payment, even knowing my moonshine, itself, was renowned. I did give him lunch, of course. He came promptly at eight and finished just before midday...and it would have taken a sizable tremor to uproot that fence now. So a decent lunch and a bottle or two of my finest would have been the least he should have expected. And I daresay that's what he'd have got if things had taken their natural course. Well, they didn't, needless to say. They couldn't have gone more disastrously, for both of us, though it was the last thing you might have thought. Petrovich became suddenly and violently ill, during lunch, and it was while wondering what to do that I suddenly realized what I'd done. It wasn't an attack of food poisoning or a bottle I'd got badly wrong. It wasn't the moonshine at all, as it happened. I'd given him sulphuric acid instead.

NINA: Oh, my God.

LOLA: Is there any reason you're doing this to yourself?

GRANNY: I can't have you thinking I'm heroic. There are causes, yes...then there are crimes.

NADIA: But it was a mistake, a genuine –

GRANNY: Oh, utterly. On his part as well. Believing it to be vodka, he downed it in one. It was only with the reaction that we realized. I did, at any rate. And then, well, you can imagine. Paralytic with horror...with fear.

NADIA: But...you did manage to save him. He recovered.

GRANNY: I need you to hear this...all of you.

NADIA: Just tell me the worst didn't happen.

GRANNY: It did. You've heard about those people who, having witnessed a murder, go into agonising detail about how badly they felt. The child-killer that weeps at the thought of his victim's suffering. I couldn't call for help.

NINA: But there was no telephone...anywhere in your street. Your neighbours were all out at work.

GRANNY: I was afraid of them laughing at me.

NADIA: Laughing at you? He was fighting for life!

GRANNY: Don't I know it! All the way to the street...clutching his throat. Then he lay there... and I watched him. (Sighs.) Have you ever seen a poisoned rat die? It takes hours.

NADIA: This is becoming unbearable.

GRANNY: Eventually, Petrovich's son found him outside their front door...still alive. And they got him to hospital quick. But by then, of course, the poison was well in his bloodstream...and he...Like that.

NADIA: I hope your neighbours held you in ridicule.

GRANNY: They did, my dear, don't worry. Petrovich, I told you, was renowned. And even though the court acquitted, my neighbours condemned me outright. I'm in prison escaping their sentence.

LOLA: But that doesn't make sense. 'Officially' –

NADIA: Does that matter?

YULIA: And I thought I was awful...for stealing a goat! Honestly, that's all I did. It was for the kids.

SHURA: My crime was even less...let me tell you. *(Beat.)* What the hell am I doing this for? *(She tosses down the material.)*

YULIA: She'll only sell it back to the screws for a huge profit...which we won't know about. I'd like to have her kidneys...boiled.

SHURA *(Rising and moving toward the dining hut.)*: Right, you gammy bitch. When are we having this porridge you been boasting about?

AMIRA *(Following.)*: I'll sort us out something better, don't worry. In a place like this, you need to know who to trust...and that's never everyone. They've been falsely suspicious of me since I came.

POLYA *(Getting up as well.)*: It's all one happy sluice bucket, you ask me.

NADIA *(To NINA.)*: I can't ask for their help now.

NINA: I think you were pushing your luck from the start. Optional hunger strikes are one thing. The food's repulsive anyway. Asking someone to do someone else's job...I'm sure some would rather put their daughters on the streets.

AMIRA *(Her voice.)*: Get out of the way, girl. You've been told what to do, and it certainly isn't this.

NADIA *(Starting off.)*: I'd better go see...

NINA: Don't provoke anybody.

JACQUI and TANYA cross to the others.

JACQUI: What do you suppose is going on over there?

MISHA: Are you getting ready to eat?

NINA: We're getting ready for a fight.

MISHA: But then I really don't understand, unless it's a joke.

JACQUI: Why should you? You just got here, like we did.

The sound of smashing crockery.

TANYA: No, nothing at all...just a prison riot.

ZHENIA (*On the verge of tears.*): She's crazy...all I did was pour tea.

AMIRA (*Her voice.*): She's useless!

LOLA (*Her voice.*): Well, then, let her be useless. What difference does it make?

ZHENIA: But I wasn't. She's just...she wants to do –

NINA: I think we all know what she's like.

AMIRA: Go on and laugh. I was just trying to help her.

JACQUI: Then why is she crying?

JADVIGA returns with a barrow of gardening implements.

JADVIGA: Well! Here they are. Anyone want to help me unload?

The women come out to see what has happened. They cross to JADVIGA with increasing interest. General: 'She was serious!'/ 'See if there's any veg.'

AMIRA: What do you think I am, your skivvy? What's going on?

GENERAL: 'What kind of seeds are they?'/ 'Does anybody remember what side they're on?'/ 'You mean idiots or whores?'/ 'What difference does it make? Just grab a spade and dig.'

AMIRA: You can't do it like that. Let me through.

YULIA: Oh, lighten up, you old sore spot.

SHURA: She probably thinks it's a trick.

AMIRA: I don't say it's anything like that, but –

LOLA: – you hate the thought of not being in charge.

The women begin selecting implements and going off to different areas. Their conversation, too, generally overlaps.

AMIRA (*To JADVIGA.*): You were a long time coming. Why was that?

LOLA: She had a lot to carry...for God's sake.

JADVIGA: I had to go for a physical.

AMIRA: Something's wrong with you, right?

SHURA: All Cinderellas submit to a physical.

AMIRA: But something's wrong with her, she said.

YULIA: We've heard you say it.

JADVIGA: Something is wrong with me.

AMIRA: You hear? You hear? (*To JADVIGA.*) Go on...tell us.

JADVIGA: They say I have gall stones. (*Hoots of laughter greet this.*) It's not funny.

YULIA (*Continuing to laugh.*): No, of course it's not, my dear. (*Perhaps an arm round her.*) Only she told us you had...

JADVIGA: Had what? Please?

AMIRA: Go on – tell them.

JADVIGA: How would you know anyway? We've never spoken.

YULIA (*To AMIRA.*): Your turn – speak up. (*Beat. To the others.*) She doesn't know a fucking thing!

AMIRA: I know who's next for the psycho ward.

SHURA: Only because you're a nark. You tell them who's next.

AMIRA: You do it yourselves, by lodging protests.

JADVIGA: Excuse me, I don't want to be the cause of any fighting between you.

SHURA: You won't be the cause, believe me.

JADVIGA: No, you don't understand. It's not right for me to have enemies when I've just come.

AMIRA: I'm not the one to make enemies.

SHURA: Ah. So you're not the one who made a point of telling us...a point of it, mind you –

YULIA: Leave it out, Shur. *(To JADVIGA.)* I think you're right.

JADVIGA: I'm going to need everyone's help with my diet.

YULIA: You're the right one to be Cinderella then. It's your job to taste the food. If anything seems too salty for you, tell us. We'll do something about it quick.

AMIRA: You might even succeed in getting veg...to plant, I mean.

JADVIGA: Oh, yes. *(Announcing it.)* She told me everybody's got to begin working their patch of soil and then, when it's good and soft, to start laying the flower seeds in very neat rows.

LOLA *(From her patch.)*: She talks as though she's never had a garden! *(To the audience.)* Anybody here with a camera? This is probably what they mean by a photo op.

JADVIGA *(To her group.)*: It feels strange giving the orders my first day.

YULIA: No doubt intended to keep you from being too friendly with the inmates.

JADVIGA: No, I told you – I want no enemies. I'm only relaying their message. *(To JACQUI and TANYA.)* Do you understand, please?

AMIRA, JACQUI and TANYA have crossed to these women.

JACQUI: But we need to ask you something.

JADVIGA: They want you also to plant...flowers, see?

JACQUI: No, that's not it.

TANYA *(Overlapping.)*: Who is it you saw, Jadviga? It could be very important to us.

JACQUI *(Overlapping.)*: She's convinced that they made a mistake.

JADVIGA: Please, girls. My English, you know, very bad.

AMIRA: They're trying to say that they're here 'by mistake'. We all by mistake, darlings. *(With a nod toward MISHA.)* They think he's here 'to help them'.

JADVIGA: Oh, yes, thanks for reminding me. Somebody told me they want to interview the two English girls.

AMIRA: That's a fucking lie!

JADVIGA: No, that's what she told me. *(To JACQUI.)* You must go when they call you.

JACQUI: Who, that guard that was here?

JADVIGA: No, it was the woman that saw me, I think it was Dr Orlova. She was a doctor anyway.

AMIRA: Yeah, her name's Orlova. *(Beat.)* Maybe they want to give you physicals.

JADVIGA: She said they'd be here some time today.

AMIRA: They're...coming here? *(General reaction.)* It's a trick, I told you. She's probably a plant.

JADVIGA: No, I give you my Bible oath – that was the mess–

MISHA *(To JACQUI and TANYA.)*: You understand? They want to talk to you here...I want to talk to you, too.

JADVIGA: He speaks English?

AMIRA: Fucking KGB fuck.

TANYA: And I don't really give a fuck. I'll talk to anyone... *(Audience.)* ... even you lot. *(Raised voice.)* You hear me? I am in-no-cent.

JADVIGA: Why you don't dig while you wait?

TANYA: Eh? What's the point? I'm getting out of here.

JACQUI: Why not plant a tree in your honour? Give them something to remember you by?

The two of them start to handle the soil. MISHA signals to JADVIGA.

JADVIGA: I've just come here. I don't want any trouble.

MISHA: And I'm head of the official delegation from Moscow!

JADVIGA *(Crossing over to him, timidly.)*: What is it you want, please?

MISHA *(Softening.)*: When you went downstairs...to the psycho ward...

JADVIGA: The where?

MISHA: So they refer to it as the hospital. Never mind. Did you hear anybody being tortured? Anybody? Anything?

JADVIGA: You're mistaken, sir.

MISHA: I'm aware how they threaten you.

JADVIGA: Don't say I was threatened...I wasn't. I just went in a shed for the tools. I heard nothing at all.

A stifled cry returns us to the cell where EVA BRAUN stands over a terrified ASKA. VALODIA stands by. EVA has a weapon.

EVA: Hit her again.

VALODIA: I'm sure she's telling the truth.

EVA: I tell you to do it. They say her husband has links with the vermin that murdered those children. You want them on your conscience?

ASKA: I haven't got a husband!

VALODIA slaps her.

EVA: But whoever did it is well-placed to murder the government. Isn't that right?

ASKA: I don't know who you... (VALODIA makes as if to slap her.) I have a brother who's in the KGB. The FSB as it is now.

EVA: There it is (To VALODIA.), you see?

ASKA: But he's nobody really. And he wouldn't tell me anyway. They don't even say who they are.

VALODIA: That's generally true. I had a schoolfriend...and for years afterwards. Nobody ever told me.

EVA: Shut up. You want us to think you're a spy?

VALODIA: I don't see the point in beating her to death. She can't tell you anything.

ASKA: Valodia's right. I haven't seen or heard from my brother in years. They're told to lose touch with their families. Mine was.

EVA: Valodia's right? *(To VALODIA.)* You were ordered to get the truth out...and you fucked her instead? I could shoot you both for high treason.

VALODIA: I'd take the gun off you. *(To ASKA.)* She's not going to shoot, sweetheart.

ASKA *(With the gun at her head.)*: I'll tell you whatever you want to know!

VALODIA grabs EVA from behind and chokes her.

ASKA: She's not dead.

VALODIA: I think she is.

ASKA: Tell me she's only unconscious.

VALODIA checks to see that EVA is dead. Then he begins dragging her off.

ASKA: Please don't treat her like that. *(He laughs.)* I'm serious. Show some respect.

VALODIA: She wouldn't have thought twice about killing you. *(Stops dragging her.)* She only just came. She won't even be missed. *(Smiles.)* You want to pray over her?

ASKA *(Sobbing.)*: I shouldn't be here!

VALODIA: That's for fucking sure.

KOMANDIR *(Her voice.)*: Has she talked yet?

VALODIA and ASKA exchange anxious looks.

VALODIA: I don't think she knows all that much, Komandir.

KOMANDIR *(Coming on.)*: That means you're afraid to find out. *(Seeing EVA sprawled out.)* What's that?

VALODIA: I thought she was one of the zeks, to be honest. She came at me with a knife.

KOMANDIR: She came at you? You're a liar. She happens to be a new guard.

ASKA: That's right, he's lying. She went crazy...came at us both with a gun. He had to do it. I'll tell them.

KOMANDIR: Shut up. There's a delegation from Moscow, out front. I'm not going to tell them one fucking thing. Neither are you, sweetheart. You're going to behave like the rest of them out there, and someone nicknamed Eva Braun, she never existed.

ASKA: She's a Jew who liked going with Germans. We...we sent her over the wall!

VALODIA: Don't worry – they'll never ask.

In the area, nearest the food hut, NADIA and ZHENIA join NINA and a gnomic GRANNY. NINA continues to work away at the material.

NADIA: Are you going to help me with the gloves, Neen? The two of us could polish off both women's quotas.

NINA: I tell you, we're better off doing no work...and Granny's right about these thermals.

ZHENIA: And I think you're right. *(To NADIA.)* There's no reason for you to do my work for me.

NINA: No sense in it either.

NADIA: You both make me sick. No, that's wrong. Forgive me. Saddened is what I feel about you. This isn't the Soviet era, all right? There's no need for quotas or time sheets or... 'doing our share'. *(Pointedly at GRANNY.)* We can afford to help our neighbour. *(To ZHENIA.)* You're right, my dear. I'm not doing it for you; I'm doing it for my own daughter.

ZHENIA: Oh. Is she...?

NADIA: If friends don't exist, there's only families...and I'm doing what I have to to look after mine. Oksana's daughter came down with meningitis and her no-good-of-a-husband left them flat. 'I got no money for wooden legs', he announced, and she brought the girl home to me. Only I couldn't do very much for the mite. So Oksana started drinking...then and more. I'd have told her to go back to Moscow if it hadn't been for Katia. Turns out that's just what I should have done. She strangled the girl by the river that Thursday, then disappeared. I haven't seen her since. My neighbours noticed both of them gone, and contacted the police. Katia's body was found. I confessed...came here. *(Starting toward the shed.)* Tell me how I'm not responsible.

A pause.

ZHENIA: I've got to go to her.

NINA: Stay here.

ZHENIA: Don't be silly. She's in there for my –

NINA: And the last thing she wants is your damned interference. Did you leave a mother at home?

ZHENIA: What does that – ?

NINA: Just answer my question.

ZHENIA: No, she died. I was placed in a hostel...the way most of us are.

NINA: But you had a mother, right?

ZHENIA: What sort of a question is that – had a mother?

NINA: When you were growing up.

ZHENIA: I don't remember. The one story they told me was that I was placed before an open window, hours after my birth. A nurse rescued me and had me placed in a hostel. Another nurse there took constant care of me. Rachel. She was Jewish. She was like Nadia...looked after me. She even tried to adopt me, take me to Israel with her. I don't know why they didn't agree to it. I left the hostel at eighteen, fit for nothing. I was due to be sent to an adult one, if I'd got a job. Somewhere I heard that Rachel was killed in an explosion...not where you'd think. On holiday, in Egypt. Lots of Russians go there these days. They're richer than Rachel could ever have been.

NINA: Want to do something for all of us do you, dear? Pretend that the stories you heard aren't true. Rachel's just the other side of the barrier...and she's planning to take you home with her...to the Promised Land.

ZHENIA: What good would that – ?

NINA: All right, insist on the truth and break a mother's grieving heart. Did your own mother die of a stroke?

ZHENIA: Stop it!

NINA: I'm fed up with the whole business. (Rises.) Where's the other slacker?

ZHENIA: Ludka? She's sleeping, I think.

NINA: Too degrading for you to do the same, I suppose. Well, why don't you dig in the garden, like Nadia wants?

ZHENIA: Couldn't I stay here with you?

NINA: I told you I'm tired of looking after you. She's right – you've less call to be here than a pregnant woman, and a letter in the right quarter would ensure that you never came back. It's a pity you never learned to write.

ZHENIA: I can write.

NINA: That's what I mean – it's a pity. *(Starts to walk with a limp.)* I've got this damned spur in my heel. Do you suppose that makes me disabled?

GRANNY: You must beat your heel hard...if you want to lose the spur.

NINA: I think I'll hang onto it...for bargaining purposes. *(Calls.)* Hey, Cinders! One of your duties is to sluice out for us!

She disappears behind the partition designated as a toilet.

JADVIGA *(To LOLA.)*: Excuse me...does that mean...?

LOLA: Go in there as soon as she's finished...and see what needs seeing to. Then you take it out back and er...do what you think should be done with it. You'll get the idea.

JADVIGA: Believe me, I do not mind...but that it should be so near the kitchens area!

LOLA: That, believe me, is the whole idea.

SHURA: ...and why we so often confuse or daily bread with our daily...you-know. (I'm watching my language for her benefit.)

JADVIGA: Why? You think Baltic women never say shit?

LOLA: She wasn't aware that you carried it, that's all.

JADVIGA: It's true. Baltic facilities are, on the whole, much better. We are in Europe now. *(She drifts off toward the toilet.)*

YULIA *(Giggles.)*: She seems really anxious to get stuck in.

LOLA: Well, there's too many of us here for one plot.

YULIA: She said groups of three.

LOLA: I count four.

YULIA: But she's gone off...Oh, you mean...

LOLA: Zhenia's here.

YULIA: I know. I just thought...she'd be watching.

SHURA (*Quickly in.*): Three's a daft number anyway. Why don't we simply pair off? There's no target, is there? All right, what's the difference?

The gardening detail is now SHURA and YULIA, LOLA and ZHENIA, JADVIGA, JACQUI and TANYA, POLYA, RAISA and AMIRA. The routine is innocuous: mulching and spreading of seeds. General: 'How far down do we go?' 'Till you find soft earth.' 'Anyone find any carrots? 'No, nothing but daffs.'

SHURA: Did they find her baby among the reeds?

YULIA: What?

SHURA: Nadia's baby.

YULIA: Her daughter's –

SHURA: Don't be stupid. She killed it. Don't ask me why, and I don't really care whose it is. But she's in here, isn't she? There's a reason, all right. Nobody's that noble or unlucky.

YULIA: I stole a goat...how unlucky is that?

SHURA (*Laughs.*): It wouldn't surprise me if she killed and cooked it for food.

YULIA: No, it was only the milk for my kids.

SHURA: What? What have your kids to do with Nadia?

YULIA: I'm talking about why I'm in here.

SHURA: Who said anything about that? I was trying to tell you how I don't believe Nadia's story. There's got to be more to it.

YULIA: But eating the baby?

SHURA: Look around you. Anyone here could be capable.

YULIA: After being in here –

SHURA: I mean before they came.

YULIA (*After looking.*): Zhenia?

SHURA: Among the most likely.

YULIA: Come on.

SHURA: I'm not arguing with you. *(Beat.)* I'm among the least likely, if it comes to that. *(YULIA laughs.)* All right, laugh. But the reason I'm in here is even less harmful, and all true. *(Beat.)* I spat in someone's face. That's all.

YULIA: You want to say you're like Zhukova or Nina protesting against the authorities.

SHURA: Less harmful, I said. Want to hear about it...or are you too much in love with your goats?

YULIA: That's –

SHURA: There was this girl that worked in our office...and she had a baby. She had a flat as well. Now that I think of it, her name was Nadia. Oh, she got on my tits something terrible. She thought she was Pavlova of the typing pool, and she hated me because I knew her for what she really was. Her eyes used to narrow like a Chink's when she passed my desk. So finally one day, I took her on. 'You're very lucky, my dear', I said, 'I often wonder if you know just how lucky you are.' 'I'm not sure I know what you mean, Aleksandra Ivanovna.' You see how she was? Baiting me, the whole time. And the whole office gawking at us...Pavlova, you see? She knew she had her audience, her adored public. So, I said, 'I just mean, my darling, that in my township, the last thing they'd reward you with is a flat. Most people have to wait twenty years...and here you are. You'd be the absolute laughing stock, I tell you. You might even find that baby of yours lying face down among the reeds. Why, they'd label you "whore" and simply spit in your face...' And – to demonstrate, yeah? – I ... *(Mimes act of spitting in Nadia's face.)* Well, that made her simply white with rage...and she stormed off into the boss's office. He must have been knobbing her himself. Maybe he only wanted to knob her. He called me in anyway, and as a result...

YULIA: As a result, what?

SHURA: I lose my job. You see?

YULIA: Not really. Who was she, this Nadia? An unmarried mother. That's nobody.

SHURA: Common as dogshit, uh-huh. That's my point.

YULIA: But you didn't kill her. Or did you? Is that why you're – ?

SHURA: Let's just drop it, all right? You obviously don't under –

YULIA: Well, no, I don't, because people aren't put into prison for –

SHURA: Oh, aren't they? Well, then, tell me my crime. Go ahead, tell me.

YULIA: I'm just saying –

SHURA: You were just milking a goat, you said.

YULIA: That's right.

SHURA: So what, did you shoot the herder that owned the goat? You must have done. That's what you're telling me.

YULIA: I did nothing!

SHURA: Well, neither did I!

A pause.

My back is killing me. Do you suppose they want us to do this all day?

YULIA: I read somewhere that if you sleep curled up, like you do as a kid, it saves your spine from hurting.

SHURA: That's very useful advice.

YULIA: I read it somewhere. Or maybe I heard it over Prison Radio.

SHURA (Overlapping.): When are we ever going to get to sleep?

YULIA: What?

SHURA: We'll probably be crippled for life before then.

YULIA (Nudging SHURA.): Hey...look.

YULIA directs SHURA'S attention to the plot where ZHENIA and LOLA are digging. What they are unaware of is the interest POLYA and RAISA are taking in them – preparing to play a trick, presumably on ZHENIA. Simultaneously AMIRA is going from group to group.

AMIRA: Care to sign the petition, my dears?

POLYA: Why don't you injure yourself?

RAISA (Giggles.): We never learned how to read.

AMIRA: Oh, but that isn't necessary. It's about the food.

POLYA: What time is dinner?

RAISA: I never got any breakfast.

AMIRA: Consider yourselves rescued, dear. She's in there this minute preparing the next fatal meal. Fatal, I tell you...she's diseased. Now I can ensure that what food we get is the best possible quality. *(Whispering.)* I have influence. That's what they say about Granny, but it's just not true. She admitted it.

RAISA: You want to move?

AMIRA: What?

RAISA: You're right where the begonias are going!

POLYA: They're daffs.

AMIRA: No, you don't seem to understand.

POLYA: Will you use your influence to tell the cook we didn't get any breakfast. Do they want us to eat the soil?

ZHENIA and LOLA are farther along, though ZHENIA is the worker. LOLA might almost be indulging her.

ZHENIA: I know it isn't the right thing to say, but I'm almost enjoying myself. It's just like working an allotment.

LOLA: They're right, you know. You shouldn't be here.

ZHENIA: Don't remind me. If someone stands lookout, I can get to the shed before they find out.

LOLA: No. You shouldn't be here. *(Of the audience.)* Ask them. Pregnant women are automatically discharged. Or those with chronic illnesses.

ZHENIA: That explains it. I was stricken before I came.

LOLA: They had no business sending you here! *(Beat.)* What did you do anyway? It can't have been serious.

ZHENIA: I stole from a shop.

LOLA: I don't believe you. You're not quick enough.

ZHENIA: I wasn't...I was caught.

LOLA: You were homeless, was that it?

ZHENIA: ...and I went into a shop.

LOLA: Guns blazing, I suppose. Have it your way. But in your shoes, I'd protest to the rafters. *(This last line is directly to the audience.)* I'd get them to bring in the TV cameras so quick, they'd think it was Beslan mark two.

AMIRA has drifted off to another area while LOLA is addressing the audience. RAISA and POLYA call to ZHENIA.

RAISA: You must have done this work before.

ZHENIA: What?

RAISA: The way it's all laid out in rows like that, neat. I'd say you've been doing it most of your life.

ZHENIA: No, not really. I'm not very far with this. I've just –

RAISA: Didn't we hear you say you had...an allotment?

ZHENIA: No, I said this was like an allotment...and we only had a small garden. It wasn't mine.

RAISA: Go on, your whole arm's as green as a meadow.

POLYA: I sure wish somebody'd help me with this.

RAISA: Help you? I've been squatting here doing everything you say!

POLYA: I mean an expert. Me and Rai are just inner-city brats...no better than gypsies really.

ZHENIA: Oh, no, it's easy. *(She starts to cross over.)*

LOLA: Hey, hold on there.

RAISA: We're only asking her advice.

LOLA: You two are doing just fine. Leave her alone.

POLYA: What're you getting so antsy about? It's not a Soviet competition, is it? Aren't we sisters?

RAISA: You keep telling her she can't do anything. I'd say that's your problem. She's great.

LOLA: I know she's –

POLYA: You don't. You keep saying she's rubbish. We heard you. 'You shouldn't be here.'

LOLA: Mind your own business.

ZHENIA: It's all right, Lo. Don't row.

LOLA: I'm not rowing.

AMIRA: I'll report how you been fighting.

LOLA: You keep your mouth shut.

AMIRA: Sign my petition then.

LOLA: Petition for what?

AMIRA: We need a new Cinderella. The Polack's diseased, and they're planning to use that to get us all transferred to the psycho ward.

LOLA: Oh, I bet. All 58 of us.

AMIRA (*Pointing to GRANNY.*): She knows. She had a look at the medicine they're planning to give us when she bartered for that cloth! They're going to lace our food with this new form of drug. The Polack's doing it right now.

LOLA: She's Lithuanian!

GRANNY: From Latvia. I wouldn't discount what she's saying, just because it's her that's saying it.

AMIRA: I got you!

LOLA: It's Amira we're talking about.

GRANNY: Exactly.

Simultaneously (and unnoticed) ZHENIA has crossed over to POLYA's and RAISA's plot.

ZHENIA: What is it you're finding so difficult? You just work the soil into a nice soft texture.

POLYA: We had a business helping people like you.

ZHENIA (*Beat.*): Then you divide it into rows.

POLYA: We may even have helped some of your friends.

ZHENIA: You have to make sure that the soil is deep enough.

RAISA: She doesn't seem to be listening.

ZHENIA: I thought you wanted help.

POLYA: Didn't you live in a hostel...for cripples?

ZHENIA: But...we're not from the same city.

RAISA: No, we advertised everywhere, didn't we?

POLYA: That's right – all over Russia.

ZHENIA: What do you mean, advertised what?

RAISA: Our company.

ZHENIA: You had a company?

POLYA: For helping cripples, yeah.

RAISA: She doesn't believe us.

ZHENIA: It's not that.

RAISA: She doesn't believe us.

POLYA: It's like this, see. We put the adverts in various papers: 'We find suitable work for crippled people...any age, any degree of crippleness.'

ZHENIA: I wish you'd stop saying that word.

RAISA: What, you think they weren't crippled?

ZHENIA: It's not a nice word.

POLYA: They weren't in the greatest condition, let me tell you. You're an Olympian gymnast, let me tell you, next to most of the ones we had. No arms or legs...the worst of them were. I don't know how they got there.

ZHENIA: And what work could you find them to do?

RAISA: Sounds difficult, doesn't it. But we managed it.

POLYA: We set them to work raising money.

ZHENIA: For charity?

POLYA: Uh-huh.

RAISA: That's right. Only some of them wouldn't cooperate, see. So we had to –

POLYA: – penalize them a bit.

RAISA: That's right, make them less greedy.

ZHENIA: I don't think I want to hear any more.

POLYA: Oh, we wouldn't have trouble with you.

RAISA: We were a business.

POLYA: How'd you like to be cheated by a bunch of –

RAISA: – armless bandits. *(Giggles.)*

POLYA: Bet you'd wish you were back in here...

RAISA: Somebody willing to do your shift.

POLYA: We had nothing like that on the outside.

RAISA: No fear. They'd take our share of the money without a qualm.

POLYA: Damned lucky they couldn't get very far.

RAISA: That's right. We'd be looking to you to make up the difference on their behalf.

POLYA: And that wouldn't have been very fair, would it.

RAISA: Lucky for you that we killed them.

POLYA: Yeah, damned lucky.

As part of the game they have blocked ZHENIA from leaving, but now NADIA has noticed and crosses over to them.

NADIA: What the hell's going on here?

RAISA: Not a thing – why?

POLYA: We was just getting acquainted.

RAISA: She was just helping us with our garden.

POLYA: Allotment expert.

NADIA (To ZHENIA.): Are you all right?

ZHENIA: Yes.

NADIA: You look like you're ready to cry.

ZHENIA (On the verge.): I'm fine.

RAISA: What, do you think we threatened her, with a knife, maybe?

POLYA: Women prisoners don't do that kind of thing.

RAISA: She thinks we're different.

POLYA: Even where we come from.

NADIA: You need to bear that in mind.

Perhaps simultaneously AMIRA approaches NINA as she returns to the compound.

NINA: You know I'm not going to sign anything, so you might just as well...

AMIRA: You'd support a hunger strike, wouldn't you? You did it when they refused Zhenia visits.

NINA: Who've you got to visit you?

AMIRA: Don't say it like that. I might have a husband like everyone else, except Zhenia.

NINA: Fine, you show me your written request and their refusal, and I'll consider –

AMIRA: That's not what I meant. Don't support me to be Cinderella, I can bear it. But don't eat the food that they cook – not after she's handled it. *(NINA sighs.)* It's a plot, I promise you. She's infected...and so will we be, one by one.

NINA: Why don't you invent some incurable disease for yourself so they'll release you? I'll back you up then. Or...I know. We can all arrange to help you over the wall to the men's zone... then you can get preggers and get released that way.

AMIRA: You don't have to tell me that all of you hate me; I felt it from the first. And I done less than any of you. I suppose that's why.

NINA: Don't be silly. We'd all like to leave here. We just want to help you.

LOLA *(To MISHA.)*: You clocked that, did you? You've got our names? Our families can expect a knock at the door in the small hours, can they? Kiss my arse!

MISHA *(Addressing LOLA.)*: Hey, Killer! What are you in for? What more can I do to you? *(Motions to silence her.)* You're all gob and no breakfast. Hear me out first, eh? We know zeks are dying off like flies, by the hour. But now someone tells us they're girls...and I mean your average Russian, not a Chechen, two eyes and a bomb up her hijaab. So, of course, now everybody's concerned. Maybe there's Chechens in charge. But I need to know all about this psycho ward. Who they have there...how long for...and how many, exactly, have never come back. *(Beat.)* What is it? Don't look at me like some western pervert or something...like we're all out here freezing to see how you girls have a slash.

DR ORLOVA, in glasses and a white coat, comes on, wheeling a trolley with an assortment of medicines. Her entrance is greeted by a frisson of interest.

NADIA: Now what do you suppose she's doing here with that?

AMIRA: I tell you because of the food...it's been tainted.

DR ORLOVA: Where can I find the new women?

AMIRA: What did I tell you? She's after the Balt.

POLYA *(Overlapping.)*: They told me they test you for crabs.

RAISA: Shout it out, why don't you.

POLYA: You'll see.

DR ORLOVA (*Consulting a clipboard.*): Apparently two Americans.

JACQUI: That must mean us.

TANYA: We're English.

DR ORLOVA: Prostitutes.

JACQUI: That must have been why we're arrested. (*To JADVIGA.*) It couldn't possibly be true, tell her.

TANYA: Kidnapped by these two gorillas....

JADVIGA: They don't speak a word of Russian, and they're terrified.

TANYA: ...and I'm not having anyone poking me...scrutinizing my discharge.

JADVIGA: She's afraid to be examined.

DR ORLOVA: Tell her this isn't a medical.

JADVIGA (*Mainly to TANYA.*): No, no, this is safe place. This woman is Dr Orlova...she is good person. I saw her in clinic with patient, very kind.

JACQUI (*To TANYA.*): You're always so arsed about everything.

TANYA: And what do you think all this is, a field trip? It's not some mistake in our reservations. We're in prison here. They sever limbs before you're released.

DR ORLOVA (*To JADVIGA.*): Tell her to shut up.

JADVIGA: You must, you know, keep mouth closed.

DR ORLOVA: They have to answer some questions. If they answer correctly, they may be released.

JADVIGA: You will need answer questions.

TANYA: My mouth's closed.

JACQUI: We'll do whatever we can.

TANYA: And we demand to see some official. You got that? *(Over-emphasising, to DR ORLOVA.)* English embassy. We want.

DR ORLOVA *(Pigeon English.)*: English whore.

JACQUI: But that's it. This is all a mistake.

DR ORLOVA *(Of MISHA.)*: And who the hell is this?

AMIRA: Someone said he's a KGB spy.

MISHA: I'm the head of a delegation from Moscow. *(To JACQUI and TANYA.)* And I speak little English.

JACQUI: I understood the word 'Moscow'.

TANYA: Then he's some kind of official. *(To JADVIGA.)* We want him to represent us, get it?

MISHA: I speak English, that is all.

DR ORLOVA: I want to question them in camera, away from Moscow's prying eyes.

JADVIGA: You have go with her...without him.

TANYA: We're not going anywhere without him.

MISHA: She does not want me.

TANYA: Then we're saying nothing. *(To JADVIGA.)* Tell her.

JADVIGA: But this is one way you can leave.

DR ORLOVA *(Showing JADVIGA photo.)*: Were they taken to this hotel?

MISHA *(Stepping in.)*: This your hotel?

JACQUI: It might have been.

TANYA: Yes, that's the one.

DR ORLOVA: And they saw this man meet with this woman?

MISHA: You saw these peoples?

TANYA: Yup. Definitely.

JACQUI: You can't be sure.

TANYA: And you were out of your face. *(To MISHA.)* She was drugged at the time.

JACQUI: You know that's not true. *(Slightly hushed.)* I'm not going to lie to get out of here.

TANYA: And you're effing daft.

JADVIGA: Both are very nervous.

DR ORLOVA: And one of them's lying. *(Distinctly.)* Hotel Peking.

JACQUI and TANYA: No!/ Yes. That's the one...and those are people we saw, absolutely. Who is he?

MISHA: He must be oligarch. *(To DR ORLOVA.)* Is that right?

JADVIGA: And they hold his girlfriend in 'psycho'. If you can know her...

JACQUI: But we don't!

TANYA: Shut up!

MISHA: What does she look like? Maybe I know her.

DR ORLOVA: That's not possible.

MISHA: But you won't object if I go with them to see her.

DR ORLOVA: They're not going. I was asked to see if the foreigners knew her, and they obviously don't.

MISHA: But you're holding someone. Why can't I see her?

DR ORLOVA *(Intimately.)*: You don't get it. It's a trick, see? They say yes, and we can hold them indefinitely.

TANYA: What's going on here?

MISHA: I try to help you.

DR ORLOVA: Look, I just told you, there's nobody.

MISHA: You just told me there was.

DR ORLOVA: But not the one you want. Forget about it.

TANYA: Will somebody tell us what's going on?

JADVIGA: I think maybe she is playing game.

DR ORLOVA: Cinderella, I want you to help with these medicines.

AMIRA: She can't do anything for you, my dear. Didn't they tell you she's a pox-ridden Balt?

TANYA (*Overlapping, to MISHA.*): Game or not, you're going to help us.

MISHA: I try to get to psycho.

TANYA: That's not good enough. We want a message delivered to the British Embassy.

For the moment, MISHA stays with the two British women while DR ORLOVA sets about distributing medicines to various members of the zone.

POLYA (*To LOLA.*): What does this mean, she tools them up?

LOLA: I wouldn't count on it, if I were you.

RAISA: We're just trying to figure out what's what.

DR ORLOVA (*Answering AMIRA.*): You think that's the same as a terrorist, do you? They give Russia maximum points during Eurovision. And I've tested her for everything going, even jaundice. She's antiseptically clean.

AMIRA: You don't understand. (*Gesturing.*) She's a plant, to inform to him. I heard them conferring earlier.

JADVIGA: That's not true, doctor. No more than my disease was.

DR ORLOVA: And what, exactly, would they be conferring about?

AMIRA: How you help certain girls with addictions, for instance.

DR ORLOVA (*Loud on purpose.*): And what about your trick of inhaling bags of sugar to make it look like a shadow on your lung?

AMIRA: What are you talking about?

DR ORLOVA: And you never complained of an ulcerous stomach?

AMIRA: And which of us hasn't?

DR ORLOVA: Do you like being put on the spot?

AMIRA: That's what I am, all right, all the time. You all know it. And I've never understood why. I'm as frightened of them as you are.

DR ORLOVA: Here's something to calm you down then. (Administers a quick injection.)

AMIRA: I didn't mean it like that.

DR ORLOVA: Anybody know where Fedina's got to?

AMIRA: You ought to give her something.

DR ORLOVA (To JADVIGA.): The backward girl...helps out in the kitchen sometimes.

JADVIGA: I've met her this morning, yes.

AMIRA: That's where she is, of course. Curled up, asleep.

DR ORLOVA: I don't think she drinks, does she, girls?

AMIRA: You mistake me. I never said 'drunk'.

LOLA: No, you just knocked her unconscious.

AMIRA: You see there? That's just what I mean. For no reason at all.

DR ORLOVA (To JADVIGA.): Do you want to fetch her in here?

On cue, LUDKA materializes.

To help us settle a long-standing dispute, Fedina. Did this woman assault you physically?

LOLA: We're all behind you, Lud. There's no need for you to be frightened.

DR ORLOVA: Shut up. (To LUDKA.) Did she hit you?

LUDKA: Hit me? No, she wouldn't dare.

AMIRA: From her own lips, you all heard it.

LUDKA: She just fixed me with her evil eye.

AMIRA: That's too silly. We all know she's mad (as a hatter).

LUDKA: Her eye, as everyone knows, is as black as coal, and her heart's like burnt cork. Of course, she fixed me. I've been under her spell for more than a week.

DR ORLOVA: And what would you like to have done to her? Burning?

LUDKA: Remove the spell.

AMIRA: I'm not going to stay here to listen...

LUDKA (*Close to manic.*): Remove the spell and beg my forgiveness.

LOLA (*And others.*): We'd all like to hear that.

LUDKA: All right, beg forgiveness from all my sisters. Go on. Let's hear you sing it, like a prayer! Make her do it, doctor.

DR ORLOVA: She'd better start saying her prayers, full stop.

AMIRA (*Trying to push past.*): Oh, go to...

DR ORLOVA: That solution I gave you a minute ago. Sodium Omeprazol. It has a strangely debilitating effect on the nervous system.

AMIRA: You said it was to calm me down.

DR ORLOVA: Mm-hm. In a very short while you'll begin to experience decline in your motor skills.

AMIRA (*Rushing out.*): Baastaards!

The compound hoots with laughter.

DR ORLOVA: That should keep her out of the way for a good while.

JACQUI: What the hell's going on here? She's going to inject every one of us?

JADVIGA: No, no...only her...who says I carry sexual disease.

DR ORLOVA (*To one or two of the other women.*): Only flour paste and salt.

TANNOY: What are you doing there, doctor?

DR ORLOVA: Making checks. Some may be seriously –

TANNOY: They go to 'psycho' if they're not well. Your job was to find out about the drugs. Did you find out?

DR ORLOVA: The English girls know nothing.

TANYA: Wait. Just a minute there.

TANNOY: And what are you doing with Moscow at your throat?

DR ORLOVA: You're the one that arranged that...aren't you?

Everyone looks up. KOMANDIR is the closest to a Soviet-era official to exist in post-Soviet Russia. She is severe in appearance and in manner. Like 'EVA BRAUN', she comes on from a height and descends to ground level. As with DR ORLOVA, there is a frisson at her entrance.

JADVIGA *(To the English.)*: She is real boss of prison. I saw her before.

KOMANDIR: I heard joyous laughter a moment ago. You think you're on holiday in Yalta? *(Someone starts to speak, but she speaks through her to TANYA.)* And you want very much to go to 'psycho', is that right? Very well!

MISHA: No! You just heard the good doctor. They don't know a thing. I'm the one you need to interview. Take me now.

KOMANDIR: Oh, yes, that's been arranged. But now what about the rest of you? You've got this looking like your private allotments.

LOLA: This is what we were ordered to do...by the new commander...Eva Braun.

KOMANDIR: I'm the only commander here. *(To DR ORLOVA.)* Is that right?

DR ORLOVA: Marina Volkanova, that's right.

LOLA: That's just what she said her name was.

KOMANDIR: Then one of us must have been lying. Care to guess which one?

LOLA: Then you don't want us for gardening detail?

KOMANDIR: I don't want you out here to shit. *(Faint mumbling.)* Any questions? I can always get the good doctor to inject the nervous among you with the same thing you pretended to give that other bitch. *(To DR ORLOVA.)* You have it for real?

DR ORLOVA *(Showing.)*: Right here, my dears.

KOMANDIR: Which one of you is Kuzina?

ZHENIA *(Inches forward.)*: Here, Komandir.

KOMANDIR: Let's see your hands.

ZHENIA: My...?

KOMANDIR *(Grabbing her hands.)*: These are lady's hands...artist's...musician's. What do you think you're showing me, art work? I want to see ulcers, like theirs! Let's see how you thread a needle. Here. *(She holds one out. ZHENIA drops it.)* Butterfingers!

NADIA: That's not fair. *(To the others.)* I don't care who she says she is.

KOMANDIR: You're not going to say it's too hard for her?

NADIA: You know the answer to that without asking.

DR ORLOVA: They call her the camp Cinderella, Komandir. She and Fedina cook and clean what they can...and take it in turn to taste the food.

KOMANDIR: But who was it who told me the new one was doing that – the diseased Balt.

This causes something of a stir among the women.

JADVIGA *(To DR ORLOVA.)*: Please tell her I'm not diseased!

NADIA *(Above the din.)*: What the fuck does it matter? We all know which of us shouldn't be here.

KOMANDIR: Excuse me! You all are here, yes? And that should mean you ought to do something. Every one of you.

NADIA: All right, but not these two. *(To the others.)* Agreed?

ZHENIA *(Speaking up and thus stopping the answer.)*: I can sew if you reduce the quota.

KOMANDIR: But why should we want to do that? (*Small murmur.*) Your crime's as severe as the others. Are you saying your sentence should be less? And how do the rest of you feel about that?

POLYA: Would that make our punishment less?

KOMANDIR: That's what she's saying.

NADIA: No, I'm not! The age of the quota is over.

KOMANDIR: And the age of the free market is here.

NADIA: And what about your observers from Moscow? (*To the audience.*) You have a view on what you've seen, haven't you?

GRANNY: But that doesn't mean they'll release her, Nadinka.

MISHA: But don't certain conditions guarantee release?

KOMANDIR: Ah. You're trying to tell us she's pregnant.

MISHA: She's Grade One Disabled. (*To DR ORLOVA.*) Isn't that right?

DR ORLOVA: I'd be very surprised if she ever worked.

KOMANDIR: So you're trying to force us to set her free?

ZHENIA: But I don't want to leave.

KOMANDIR: All right, she's free.

MISHA: But you're not serious.

KOMANDIR: What do you want, a sworn affidavit? (*Of LUDKA.*) What about her?

LUDKA: Why is she pointing at me? (*To KOMANDIR.*) You have raven's eyes!

LOLA (*Stepping in.*): Shh, shh , shh...It's all right, Lud. She's entitled to do that. She's the boss.

LUDKA (*To DR ORLOVA.*): Can you give her something to make her stop?

DR ORLOVA: That's right. I'll give her something, don't worry. Sleeve? (*Prepares to inject LUDKA.*)

LUDKA: No, not me. Her.

DR ORLOVA *(To KOMANDIR.)*: She'll go to sleep in a minute or two.

LOLA: For how long? *(Looking round.)* I hope all of you noticed what just happened here. *(To MISHA.)* Did you?

MISHA: I saw it, all right. *(To KOMANDIR.)* Where does she go now, the 'psycho' ward?

DR ORLOVA: She goes back where she goes every night...and half the days. *(To LUDKA.)* Go on now, dear. You're all right.

LUDKA *(Going out.)*: And you'll make sure that nobody follows me?

DR ORLOVA: Perfectly sure, dear. I'll be standing guard.

LUDKA *(Going off.)*: There's a dagger of vengeance right by my side.

Everyone watches.

MISHA *(To DR ORLOVA.)*: And what happens next? One day you'll give her enough so she won't wake up?

NADIA *(To ZHENIA.)*: You see why we're anxious to get you out of here?

ZHENIA: I do, but... *(She looks at KOMANDIR.)*

NADIA: She's afraid of the same thing happening to her. *(To ZHENIA.)* Is that right?

KOMANDIR: What, with Moscow staring down our gullet? *(Looking round.)* I don't want her here! The other one, all right. You can put her to sleep. But you're a pain in the butt cracks. Create tensions. Everybody taking sides...before even nine in the morning. Oh, get her out of here, please.

ZHENIA: But where would I go?

DR ORLOVA: With me, to sign the release forms.

ZHENIA: No, you don't understand.

KOMANDIR: If she stays here, she works the full quota. There's no other way.

ZHENIA: All right, then, I'd just as soon die here, among the people I've known. You're as much family as I've ever known. If I leave, I'll be homeless. And then, back inside, somewhere else.

POLYA: If we were out, we could find her a place to stay.

RAISA: That's right...and a job to do.

ZHENIA: You see? I'll end up like...their friends.

RAISA: What's the matter with that? They're at peace now.

POLYA: One room to a customer.

NADIA: And that's not going to happen to you. (To POLYA and RAISA.) You're in here for a long time to come.

POLYA: Oh, we have loads of friends on the outside.

NADIA: So's Nina. (NINA perks up at the mention of her name.) You're from Zhenia's home town, aren't you, Neen? Close enough anyway.

NINA: Yeah, sure. All my nieces and nephews...the brothers that are still alive.

NADIA: And surely somebody be happy to take you in.

NINA: Oh, yes, I can give you my Tanya's address right now.

KOMANDIR: There's time enough for that later on. Are we all right now? I want this sorted and everybody back to the jobs they were meant to be doing before they got out here this morning.

LOLA: And what happened to Eva?

JADVIGA: What do you want me to do?

KOMANDIR: Which one are you, the drug dealer's whore? Oh, no, you're the Balt whore.

JADVIGA: I'm from Latvia.

DR ORLOVA (Reaching out to ZHENIA.): And you come with me, my dear.

MISHA: Hang on just a second. (To KOMANDIR.) She's taking her off...to the 'psycho' ward?

KOMANDIR: You mean to say Moscow disapproves?

DR ORLOVA: I already told you, there's no oligarch.

MISHA: That's right. You said it's a trick.

NADIA: No, she's being released. You helped to secure it.

MISHA: I just want to know how many others you're holding.

KOMANDIR: How many others we've tortured to death? Feast your eyes!

Tableau of VALODIA and ASKA together. During what follows, ZHENIA goes off with DR ORLOVA.

ASKA: Misha!

MISHA: It is you. (*Of VALODIA.*) Who's this? (*To VALODIA.*) If you laid one fingertip on her, you bastard, I'll –

ASKA: No, no, you don't understand. Valodik has been my protector.

MISHA: Protector, my arse. He's a prison thug.

VALODIA: And she's in here, I guess, only because of you.

MISHA: I'll kill (you).

VALODIA: It's okay by me. I was only asked to find out what she knew.

ASKA: And I could tell them next to nothing...

KOMANDIR: So now we're planning to release her, too, like the other one, unscathed. Without a blemish, in fact.

MISHA: Because you figure you got me. Your quack called it a trap.

KOMANDIR: In front of how many witnesses? You didn't ingest anything, did you? Orlova never injected you.

VALODIA (*Laughing.*): And the last thing I want is to wrestle you to the ground. I think you owe her some kind of line, even if you do it in private.

ASKA: I don't want you to tell me anything, Misha. I don't know anything, as I told them. And I want to keep it that way. I want you to tell me if you're all right, only. It's even all right if you lie. I'll still know.

MISHA: I'm not all right, no.

ASKA: What?

MISHA: I could scarcely be worse and still be alive. (*Addressing the audience.*) All my colleagues out there think I'm spying on them – I'm the one under surveillance. Ask them! I must know when and where the next Chechen attack comes? You're asking the wrong man!

ASKA: Oh, I'm so relieved. (*Matching his hands on the fence.*) Oh, Mishenka!

MISHA: What's the difference? They still think I know.

VALODIA: You might just as well finger me. I was at Beslan and the theatre siege. Chechen lady had her bullet thrower dead on me. I thought I'd be killed because she didn't shoot.

ASKA: I don't care...I'm not bothered about anything now. You're alive...you're not injured... and they can keep me in here for however long –

Suddenly over the tannoy there is the piercing sound of someone in pain. It freezes the action for a long moment.

LOLA: What the fuck was that? There's nobody out there.

ASKA: You're quite wrong.

LOLA: Eva Braun?

ASKA: She died an hour ago. He killed her. And then she (*Of KOMANDIR.*) told him to hush it up.

VALODIA: But I did that to stop her from killing you.

The scream is repeated.

NADIA: You bastards! (*She moves toward the KOMANDIR, but VALODIA blocks her way.*)

KOMANDIR: That's right. Keep her there. (*Calling out.*) Orlova!

NINA: I think somebody ought to tell us what's going on.

ASKA: I tell you they're torturing someone.

KOMANDIR: Not you. (*To DR ORLOVA.*) Can you tell them, no one's been tortured?

DR ORLOVA: It's all right. I promise you, everything's...

NINA: What was that scream then, rusty pipes?

DR ORLOVA: I give you my word – your friend's perfectly safe.

NADIA: Bring her here then.

DR ORLOVA: I can't...at the moment.

NADIA: Why not, if you say she's all right? Bring her to us!

VALODIA: You know I don't want to hurt anyone.

NINA: Nadia, dear, everything's for the best...whatever happens.

POLYA: I don't see what you're worried about. We all heard her say that she'd sooner die here.

Suddenly NADIA lunges at POLYA with a sharp gardening implement. The move catches everyone off-guard. Then several move in to pull NADIA off POLYA. Detaching herself from the action, LOLA addresses the audience.

LOLA: Well! What does that make it now? Three killings inside the women's zone? That's unheard of! And what's Moscow going to say?

Instant blackout.

Author's note

There is a veritable library of documentation about Russian prison life. I am particularly indebted to Irina Ratushinskaya and her memoir *Grey is the Colour of Hope* (Hodder and Stoughton: 1986) for the general ambience of prison life in this play. The characters, their stories and individual behaviour are, creatively, mine.

EMIGRÉS

A Grotesque Comedy

Workshopped as part of a second-year module by Drama students of the University of Exeter in January 2005, under the direction of Martin Harvey and with the following distribution of parts for the various scenes:

IMMIGRATION OFFICER	Matthew Lockwood
TANYA	Laura Sibbick/Ginny Henning/Megan Atkin/Jenny Barbrook/ Liz Norwalk
INDIAN	Laura Kerr
MAKSIM	James Louis/Tim Schofield/Mark Evans/Tom Armstrong/ Peter Lawrence
ROY	Patrick Godin
ANNA	Nancy Scott
INNA	Eeva Hautala
BRANGWEN	Megan Atkin
BEZNIK	David Dimitriou
BETTY	Nancy Scott
OLIVER	Jamie Williams
MISS HIGHLIGHTS/FRANKLYN	David Dimitriou
McBRIDE	Matthew Blackhurst
NATALYA	Laura Kerr
POLBOI	James Anniballi
ALENKA	Carys Stephen
MARTINS	Matthew Lockwood
SCOOBY	Martin Harvey

Various places in the West Country (Act One) and in Scotland (Act Two).

ACT ONE

Unit set representing various locations mainly in the West Country and in Scotland. The fluid nature of the scene changes should have some suggestion of dreams. MAKSIM is dark-haired and thin, TANYA is blonde and tiny. Their first encounter is with an Immigration officer. In general, when foreign characters speak in accented, broken English, it's assumed that they are trying to speak English. When their speech is normal, it's to be assumed that they are speaking in their own language.

IMMIGRATION: You and your...

TANYA: He's looking at me funny. Can you get him to stop it?

IMMIGRATION: Is something the matter?

MAKSIM: ...wife. She's my wife. There's something the matter with her eyes.

IMMIGRATION: We call that shifty. *(Looks down at documents.)* You came from the Ukraine.

MAKSIM: She...she is Ukrainian. We came from Kaliningrad.

IMMIGRATION: Isn't that part of a Baltic republic? It's almost Euroland. How can you say you've been persecuted? Are you on the run? *(He consults a file.)*

MAKSIM: I'm a trained barrister. *(A beat.)* You can tell by my knowledge of English...can't you? My wife's a registered nurse, back in Russia.

IMMIGRATION *(To TANYA.)*: How is your English, dear?

TANYA: I little speak. Learn. Learn. Blakha-mukha. *(To MAKSIM.)* Tell him you're teaching me.

IMMIGRATION: Try telling her not to profane.

MAKSIM: She didn't say...

IMMIGRATION: 'Blacka...' something.

MAKSIM: It means nothing. Gibberish.

IMMIGRATION: So you say. She could be laughing at me while I grin like a Butlins rep. *(A beat.)* Before too much longer, you characters will have to apply for asylum before leaving.

MAKSIM: What does that mean...that you're sending us back?

IMMIGRATION: I may have a love child in Bucharest...where she's likely to grow up under-advantaged. *(Stamps document hard.)* And I'm a permanent civil servant. Don't you think I'm entitled to special consideration? *(Handing him documents.)* Report to the detention centre at Harrow.

MAKSIM: What about our passports?

IMMIGRATION: We keep them safe. *(Holds out vouchers.)* Give you these vouchers instead. *(Beat.)* You think you're entitled to anything better? If you'd have said you lost these, we would have sent you back...within the hour.

Indian checkout worker (woman) confronts TANYA about her purchases.

WOMAN: Tights and sanitary towels aren't on the list.

TANYA: I sorry. Little spik English.

WOMAN: You cannot get tights and sanitary towels with your vouchers – *(As if to a deaf person.)* It's not allowed.

MAKSIM approaches them.

TANYA *(To MAKSIM.)*: Did you hear that? She's not English. *(To the WOMAN.)* Don't they have feminine hygiene in your country?

WOMAN: She can blaspheme as much as she likes, tell her.

MAKSIM: She's not blaspheming.

TANYA *(Almost in tears to the WOMAN.)*: Nids this panties, understand? I nids.

WOMAN; They're not pants, for a – *(To MAKSIM.)* Will you tell her they're not underwear?

MAKSIM: She knows what they are; she just doesn't know the English.

WOMAN: I'm not having this conversation, right? Vouchers are only for the essentials. A s.t.'s is not an essential.

MAKSIM: I agree with Tanya – you don't have periods in this country?

WOMAN: I'll call the manager – say you've been sexually harassing me.

MAKSIM: Call him, yes, fine. Then we can get what we want.

WOMAN: Nobody ast you to come here, did they. Shouldna come if you don't wanna follow the rules.

TANYA: I'll put them back where I found them. *(To WOMAN.)* Tek back, you see? *(Under her breath.)* Blakha-mukha.

WOMAN: Give them back. I don't trust you. *(Beat.)* My family came in the fifties. You think we had it right? Filled my knickers with dogshit my first week at school...and we was jolly-just-come, just like you. *(Beat.)* Tell her to use toilet paper.

ROY WINTERS taps TANYA on the shoulder. She gives a start.

ROY: Can I have a word with your husband? We have various folk to look after you.

TANYA: Excuse, please. I little spik.

ROY: Oh, God. Are you both in the same boat? Kosovan? We have three of you staying here at the moment.

TANYA: Rossian. From Rossia.

ROY: That's wonderful. There's nobody here who speaks...

MAKSIM: I speak English.

ROY: Are you sure? Wonderful, right. That's a miracle. Well. You won't need the vouchers in Devon. The Government pays us for each of you, bed and board. You're free to look for whatever work you can find. But that may be no better than the poultry farm outside Newton Abbot. Or if you and your wife want to stay together, there's always the meal shifts here. My name's Roy Winters, by the way. Like the season, and with an 's'. Celestine, the guy doing it now, is a gift from the gods, but he's also from darkest Africa, and the Kosovans won't touch a thing he cooks. He scrubs up better than they do, twice a day. But I keep thinking they'll hack him like they hack the heads off their 600 daily cocks and hens. You might help to prevent an axe murder, fancy that.

ANNA buttonholes TANYA, her speech overlapping with ROY'S.

ANNA: Is he off again, like he's trying to get some chamber of something-or-other to leave their fortunes with us for Whitsun week. I be his second wife, Anna, and his first Brangwen was Welsh, if you can picture the gabby pair they made.

ROY: ...and she doesn't speak any English.

ANNA: ...and so you're telling me that he does? It's that rare when I has a woman to talk to. *(To TANYA.)* We do get the odd married couple, like yourselves. But mostly they're daughters of Allah, which is very odd, indeed. You never see hide nor hair even when they're right there in front of you...and as for airing their thoughts –

ROY: Have you even asked her name?

ANNA: A simple smile communicates volumes. *(To TANYA.)* He's referring to the fact that this used to be an old people's home, and I never talked to any of the old dears. *(To ROY.)* This one's as young and as bright as somebody's little sister...

MAKSIM: My wife's name is Tanya.

ANNA: What did I tell you?

ROY: They want to be left alone.

The couple start out, but their progress is blocked by BRANGWEN with another resident, INNA.

BRANGWEN *(Accented and in mid flow.)*: ...expect you could do with a long sit-you-down.

ANNA: Brangwen!

BRANGWEN: And you must be wondering what I think I'm doing.

ANNA: You was here once upon a winters. Now I seem to recall it's somewhere else, in town.

BRANGWEN: The man at the station didn't know that, you see. When this woman here struggled to say Winters Rest, he got hold of me on the run. On my way to Whipton Village, I was, only what could I do? She needs help.

ROY *(To MAKSIM.)*: She didn't train in with you?

MAKSIM: We never saw her before.

BRANGWEN: From one platform to the next and the one after that, she's been missing her connections all day long. Right the way down to Cornwall, she could have been. And her tears alone told me that. She can't speak a word of good English.

ANNA: One more waif and stray.

BRANGWEN: It's my idea she's some sort of Russian.

TANYA (*Lighting up, to INNA.*): Russia? You're from Russia?

INNA (*Lighting up.*): Thank you, God. Someone who speaks my language.

TANYA: Of course, yes, we're from Zhitomir.

INNA: I'm sure He's been watching over me.

MAKSIM: We're not really Ukrainian.

INNA: ...I have in-laws in Uter-Mylovsk'.

BRANGWEN: I've a notion they're known to each other.

ROY: Are you going to let us get to bed?

ANNA: They'll need towels and a fresh set of bedding...each.

BRANGWEN: And don't forget the food now.

ROY: Betty's gone home for the evening.

BRANGWEN: But I'm yere.

ANNA: She's getting her feet back under the table.

BRANGWEN (*Moving toward the kitchen.*): Just tell me what there is to eat.

ANNA: I'll do whatever wants doing.

ROY: Why can't we all just be friends?

ANNA: The Mormons is settled in Utah, my own love. Your decree puts you firmly with me, alone, under the one roof.

BRANGWEN: Of course, yes, I'm on my way home.

ANNA: Has she pitched tent out in the garden or something?

BRANGWEN: I don't want the least little fuss now.

ROY: She didn't ask to come this evening.

ANNA: Is it all right? I'm asking her to leave.

Overlapping with this.

MAKSIM: We actually came from Kaliningrad.

TANYA: His sister lives there.

INNA: I've never lived anywhere else but Bryansk.

MAKSIM: We went through there the year before last.

INNA: How long have you lived in this country?

MAKSIM: Forty hours.

TANYA: They kept us in Harrow last night.

MAKSIM: Did you fly to Heathrow from Moscow?

INNA: It seems like a month in the train. I changed at Harrow and nearly caused a panic when I crossed the tracks on foot.

TANYA: God in heaven.

MAKSIM: The rail's electrified.

TANYA: She wouldn't know that.

INNA: Of course not, in Russia it's dead.

MAKSIM: They must have thought they were watching a suicide.

INNA: With my luggage?

MAKSIM: Minor detail.

TANYA: It's very strange.

INNA: At Harrow in someplace called Tesco's –

TANYA: ...you used vouchers.

INNA: I hit a man. He started putting my things in his shopping bag, so I got him to stop. How could I know he was trying to help me?

MAKSIM: How could he know she was Russian?

INNA: His face like this... (Shows horror.) ...and the woman behind grabbed my arm. Someone else was beginning to ring the police, but then the first man explained.

TANYA: Embarrassed to tell you what happened to us.

Suddenly someone outside throws a brick through the window. The alarm goes off and doors open upstairs. Several male shouts further orchestrate the disturbance.

BEZNIK (Off, heavily accented.): Somebody trying to kill us!

ROY (Calling up the stairwell.): It's all right. It's only the local booze brigade saying goodnight on the way home. Happens two or three times a month, and it's nothing personal.

ANNA: Should you be putting it to them precisely in those terms?

ROY: What, you want to start a vendetta?

BRANGWEN: Would you consider seeing me home?

INNA (To TANYA.): Ground-floor windows in Russia are fitted with iron bars.

TANYA (To MAKSIM.): Are we going to stay here?

MAKSIM: You think we should go back to Harrow...maybe Kaliningrad?

ROY: I tell you everything's all right. You're perfectly safe.

Police siren sounds.

MAKSIM: Excuse me, please. But this is the kind of thing we thought we were escaping by coming to Britain.

ROY: Well, what do you want me to do about it?

TANYA (To INNA.): My husband's a lawyer.

ROY: It's my broken window, not yours.

Lighting shift.

Kitchen. BETTY, wizened and 60ish, is talking to INNA as they both prepare food. BEZNIK, Kosovan, is trying to chat up TANYA, peeling spuds.

BETTY: You must stop me if I'm speaking too quickly or...or quickly, that's right.

INNA: I little understand.

BETTY: That's a problem for most of us, in a place such as this. And I was here in the days when they looked after old folks.

INNA: Sorry.

BETTY *(Loudly.)*: I'm saying it used to be a Home.

INNA: This is not home? I don't understand.

BETTY: You don't get it, my dear. Not a home like in 'house', but like in old people's home...for people that can't look after theirselves.

INNA: Hospital?

BETTY: No! I mean, something like. Only not the same thing...you know – different.

INNA: Difficult, English language. Many meanings same word.

BETTY: Well, there's not many as would confuse house for a nursing home. Or a hospital.

INNA: Hospital have nurses in England...or no.

BETTY: You're not just being clever, are you? *(Ire rising.)* I said an old people's home!

INNA: What means 'clever'?

BETTY: Smart-arse...

INNA: ...'arse'?

BETTY: Ask your English teacher, dear. I ent no genius. Only don't ask him that, for God's sake. He'll think you been mixing with the wrong sort of people.

INNA: Russia language one word for one thing.

BETTY: That's all right – spare me the Russian for...It's your reverse side, you know – this. *(Turns and touches her bottom.)*

INNA: Russia people show to people they don't like.

BETTY: They don't! Amazing, that is. It's almost the meaning of 'smart-arse', and we've barely a sentence to say to each other! When's your birthday? I can make you a chocolate cake.

Overlapping.

BEZNIK: I try spikking English for you. My name Beznik, you know? Bez-nik? From Kosovo. Parents kill by Serbia bastard. Sister rape. You like the whiskey? Johnnie Walker red.

TANYA *(Low tone in 'her own tongue'.)*: You couldn't be from Kosovo, no. I don't believe it. Your eyes are blue. *(To BEZNIK, with gestures.)* Your eye...very! *(Pointing to her own eye.)* Very.

BEZNIK *(Grinning.)*: My eye, yes, very!

TANYA: Very! I mean...how?

BEZNIK: Your name?

TANYA: My eye is blue, of course! *(Lower tone.)* What does he think? I'm a natural blonde.

BEZNIK *(Idiot slowly.)*: What is your name, please?

TANYA: Tanya. Tatiyana.

BEZNIK: That is 'very'.

TANYA *(Responding in kind.)*: Most women in Russia.

BEZNIK: What? *(Grinning.)* Your name? Fantastic. Russia drink vodka. We drink Russia vodka to Russia women – okay? Russia vodka...Stolichnaya. Okay?

TANYA: Russia vodka...okay.

BEZNIK: You, me and...your boy together drink.

TANYA: 'Boy'? You mean my husband? *(Deliberately.)* You know the meaning of 'husband'? Married...boy...man and me.

BEZNIK: I go finding wife very day.

TANYA *(Low tone.)*: You think you're going find her through me? *(To him.)* All right...I go now... Bye-bye. *(Starting off.)*

BEZNIK: You want drink now, upstairs?

TANYA: I'm off to get my husband, you pervert. You keep out of my way. *(Fending his arm away.)* No, no...no touch me – I'm married, see? *(Shows her ring finger.)* Innochka, quick. Over here.

INNA: What is it?

TANYA: Safety in numbers.

BETTY watches them and addresses BEZNIK.

BETTY: We meant to warn you about this one. *(Sternly.)* Beznik. You pack it in, you hear me? Mr Roy speaks louder than I do. Do you want to hear it from him?

BEZNIK *(Corresponding tone.)*: I don't want to marry you, old lady. No England passport, no, thanks.

BETTY: I never asked you to marry me, you perfect loon. I'm talking about these here girls. You're not to speak to them, hark to me? Or smile, or just about nod. They're off limits to you in any dimension, and I'm not bothered if you can't catch my every word. You get my meaning, I'm sure, very clearly, and if you don't, we can circulate Mr Roy.

TANYA *(To INNA.)*: You don't smell something burning, do you?

INNA: Burning?

TANYA *(Rushing to the big oven.)*: My God – it's the whole roast. *(Angrily, to BETTY.)* You kept us talking so much, it's all burnt.

INNA: How could it be Betty's – ?

The smoke alarm goes off.

TANYA *(Showing food.)*: You see it? There's nothing left....and Roy will ask us to pay for it. Maybe dock us some wages or...withdraw our food. You're my witnesses, eh? *(To BETTY.)* I'm going to tell him it's all your fault.

BETTY: I don't get a word what you're saying, dear. I know you're very angry about something...

TANYA *(To BETTY.)*: Crazy...you are... *(Touches her temple.)*

BETTY: Because I tried to protect yer? I thought you needed help.

INNA: You can't talk to someone like that – it's very rude.

BETTY: He was going to merlest yer.

TANYA *(Thrusting the tray of food at BETTY.)*: You want the bitch? All right then, have it. Go on. Eat it yourself...off the floor. Senile...somebody ought to put the bitch down.

The food falls to the floor. INNA bends down to pick it up.

Let her lick it up. It's what she wants. *(To BETTY, pointing.)* You go...like dog.

INNA: Your language gives me a headache. Please stop.

BETTY *(Tearfully.)*: I was only trying to help yer.

INNA: Beznik, help, please.

BEZNIK *(Eagerly, coming forward.)*: Yah, what, darling lovely, I help.

INNA goes for a mop to try to shut off the alarm with the mop handle. BEZNIK eagerly grabs hold of her waist.

TANYA: Why don't you bring the bucket for the floor?

BETTY: I'd do anything for you to forgive me. Only please tell me what I done wrong.

TANYA *(Waving her hand as though she's trying to wave away an insect.)*: Blakha-mukha... can't she get the point?

INNA *(Trying to show him.)*: You must...like this...do.

BEZNIK *(Laughing, holding tighter.)*: Like this?

INNA *(Flaring.)*: I am not lovely darling for you...I am witches! I keel you. Understand?

BEZNIK *(Angry.)*: Fine, okay, fuck you very much. Fuck you.

Smoke alarm upstairs goes off. Voices off seem to echo the level of disturbance here. Doors open noisily. ANNA remonstrates before coming on with MAKSIM.

ANNA: You think you can do what you like in this house?

MAKSIM: When the food is as awful as this is, I do, yes. It becomes a necessity.

ROY: What the hell's going on?

ANNA: There's a thing here called fire regulation – with a £1,000 fine attached.

INNA manages to stop the alarm in the kitchen when ROY, MAKSIM and ANNA come on. The upstairs alarm stops shortly afterwards, followed by a slamming bedroom door.

ROY: So you're saying it wasn't by mistake?

ANNA: What wasn't? A bloody barbecue in the bathroom? He has to be some sort of deranged.

MAKSIM: It's raining outside.

ANNA: And if it wasn't?

MAKSIM: We'd have it outside.

ROY: W-wait a minute. (To MAKSIM.) She's serious – a barbecue?

BETTY: That's exactly what we had in here.

ROY: Yeah, but I mean like...how?

INNA (To TANYA.): You don't know what they're talking about, do you?

TANYA: It must be the fire alarm.

INNA: But we'd have become mad. Are they saying I did wrong?

TANYA: Not this one, Innochka...something to do with Maksim.

MAKSIM (Overlapping, to ROY.): Three days ago in Tesco. It would have gone off another day.

ROY: But how in the loo did you cook it? And why?

MAKSIM: The standard of hygiene is very poor.

ANNA: Pardon?

MAKSIM: A Primus stove.

TANYA: Do you want to tell us what's going on?

INNA: Just tell me I'm not to blame.

ROY: Overlooking the obvious insult, my wife is right – it's against regulations.

MAKSIM: Nothing happened, did it?

BETTY: They're saying I burnt the roast.

MAKSIM (After glancing at BETTY.): That's exactly why I did it.

ANNA: We could take you to court.

MAKSIM: Fine, you do that...I'll take you on.

ROY: I've had dealings with barrack-room lawyers before. In the Army. That's what we called you geezers that thought you knew everything and sounded off whenever you could. Always threatening to take us to court, you were.

MAKSIM: I never threatened – you asked me why.

ROY: Well, now I'm asking you to –

MAKSIM: You also asked us to help you avoid a blood bath. At £1.50 an hour, £5 daily for Tanya? That's you...avoiding the minimum wage. We had wages like that back in Russia.

ANNA: So what are they doing in this country? Ask him.

ROY: There's always the poultry farm.

MAKSIM: You think we wouldn't consider it? You've got us working three shifts. How much are you getting for each of us?

ROY: Less than I'm paying you.

MAKSIM: How do we know? And what, exactly, are you giving us for it? (Looking at BETTY.) Food we can't eat...by a woman who must have been one of the inmates before. You can't even give us a double room, and the beds, with their plastic sheets, must have been used by the inmates as well. They smell like it. Tanya looked after people like her back in Russia. Now you're asking us to work with her? It cannot be done.

BETTY: He's not talking about me, is he?

ROY: You don't hear anyone else sounding off.

MAKSIM: No, of course. To slaughter poor chickens is easier.

BETTY: Does he know what his own wife was doing before – with that one? *(Points to Beznik.)* And look what he's doing now to Inna.

BEZNIK *(Grins.)*: We good friends...Russia–Kosovo.

INNA removes his hands from her waist.

TANYA: I wish I understood what you're telling them.

MAKSIM *(To ROY.)*: I could report you to the Home Office on several counts.

ROY: And Strasbourg...could you?

MAKSIM: Of course, but London's enough.

ROY: All right then, try it.

MAKSIM: Exploitation...sub-standard living conditions.

ROY: Yeah, you told me. Have a go.

INNA *(Hushed, to TANYA.)*: I don't like it. They both look...

TANYA: You're not going to hit him, are you dear?

INNA: Roy could call the police...and he's bigger and stronger anyway.

TANYA *(Moving to stop him.)*: Please don't, Maksim.

MAKSIM: I'm not going to touch him, don't worry.

TANYA: Well, then come back upstairs. *(Trying to lead him off.)* Come on.

ROY: I figured you'd bottle out in the end.

MAKSIM: Will you give us a room of our own anyway?

ROY *(Barks laughter.)*: Why should I?

MAKSIM: ...two single rooms and we're married.

ROY: No, I mean where's your threat? How much teeth have you really got? Strasbourg! You're two trouble-makers, that's all. Pains in the arse. I'd rid myself really if you weren't around. And where else, exactly, are you going to go? *(Starting off.)* If there's nothing else you want to whinge...

MAKSIM: We could leave here tomorrow.

ROY: And I'd be straight on the phone. Obliged to report it, aren't I? Violation of terms. They'd get after me for that, sure. I could go to gaol for not reporting you...I'd almost certainly get the chop.

ANNA: What on earth are you saying – who's going to gaol?

ROY: Our legal beagle reckons he's nailed me.

ANNA: I want you both to stop this. It's not at all nice.

ROY: It's not at all anything, my love. That's why I can't be arsed. But if you think you got hold of something, as I say...Give us a laugh.

BEZNIK: I want us all drink.

Lights begin to fade except on TANYA and on INNA, picked out by spotlight. The others are frozen in shadow.

TANYA: Maksim explained it to me upstairs. He's really angry with Roy, and the way he explained it...there's no going back.

INNA: What do you mean? Betty's really a good person. You made her cry after you left.

TANYA: I can't talk about that now – we're leaving.

INNA: You can't do that.

TANYA: Maksim says we can...we must, in a way.

INNA: What 'must'?

TANYA: What all that was about today. If no one knows where we're going, Maksim says, what can they do? Maksim says he's in touch with a man who can give us a job and a resident permit.

INNA: I don't believe it.

TANYA: I can't argue with you. *(A beat.)* They turned down our application.

INNA: But you can appeal.

MAKSIM *(Shouting to ROY.)*: I'm not going to take any more of it!

ROY: You're barking.

TANYA: On what grounds? This is a genuine offer, you see? A job and a residence permit. Maxim's a lawyer, Inna. Who's going to cheat us? He's worked for oligarchs.

INNA: I don't want to know any more. Don't.

TANYA: I can't say any more. I don't know it. Except...I'll keep in touch.

Lighting shift. Everyone but TANYA and MAKSIM leave the space and OLIVER takes ROY'S place when the lights come up again.

OLIVER: We cater for a kind of ex-collusive clientele. I don't mean they're funny peculiar. But we've only the twelve *en suite chambres*, you see? And we date back to Tudor times/look at the beams. Do you know about 'Murder Weekends'? Themes like that for the paying guests. Well, we don't go into any of that, thank you. I'm not averse to hearing we have the odd ghost, that can add to the overall *élan* as long as it's not taken to extremes/you said you were what nationality?

MAKSIM: Russian.

OLIVER: Does your little friend speak? *(To TANYA.) Bonjour, ma petite.*

MAKSIM: Does she speak what, English, you mean?

OLIVER: Well, yes. But if she doesn't, it's a fair bet she's not going to say much at all. At least nothing the rest of us can understand. What's she saying now, for example? (Point to me, I think.)

MAKSIM: Tanya and I are married, by the way.

OLIVER: That's exactly our sort of guest – marrieds. Young or old, but they come to us attached, if you catch my deeper meaning. One word says it all, like the most succinct holiday brochure. One look and you know we don't readily welcome pets or large family or anything one might describe as brash. So if you think you'd be happy to join us...

MAKSIM: You talked of a resident permit.

OLIVER: Oh, yes, you said Russian, didn't you. We've had an assortment of Asians working for us, Orientals...

MAKSIM: You're not racist, are you?

TANYA (Hushed voice.): He looks to me like a blue boy.

OLIVER: Is that what it sounds like, Russian? It must be colourful.

TANYA: I've heard it's the English disease. I think we should go somewhere else.

OLIVER: Wait a moment – we had a Yusipov staying here at one time. I think it might be an omen, don't you? We can try it out anyway, all of us, and if we find we're not a match...

MAKSIM: What about salary?

OLIVER: Well, now, which do you want answered first? 'Am I racist?' If they've worked here, how can I be? You want a resident-something or other. Why? Is England a police state?

MAKSIM: We came in as asylum seekers! We need permission in order to stay!

OLIVER: I hear perfectly out of both ears.

MAKSIM: I'm sorry. Chinese and Asians have worked here. Were they deported?

OLIVER: They moved on by their own choice, as I remember. Does £5 an hour appeal to you? That was your third point.

MAKSIM: Is that for each of us?

OLIVER: You like? I told you the kind of people we have here. Nothing about us is cut-rate.

MAKSIM (To TANYA.): He said we can have £5 each an hour... (To OLIVER.) ...for how many hours?

OLIVER: To start with? Seven-to-ten thirty, midday-to-six.

MAKSIM (To TANYA.): Eight and a half hours, finish at six.

TANYA: I don't think that's possible. Hotel work isn't like that. Think about it. We're servants. We work different hours to other people.

OLIVER: What's your name, dear?

TANYA (*To MAKSIM.*): What's – ? (*To OLIVER.*) My name?

OLIVER: Ah, she understands that much. Ex-cellent.

TANYA: Tanya.

OLIVER: Ex-quisite.

TANYA (*To MAKSIM.*): I want to leave.

MAKSIM: No, let's try it for a while anyway. (*A beat.*) Where else are we going to go? Tonight?

TANYA: Has he talked about what kind of rooms they're giving us?

MAKSIM: One room, I think it is. (*To OLIVER.*) And we'd be living where?

OLIVER: A studio. Downstairs.

MAKSIM (*To TANYA.*): That's right...in the basement.

OLIVER: There was a Tanya in *Eugene Onegin*, wasn't there?

TANYA (*To MAKSIM.*): Why can't we live outside?

MAKSIM: Outside where? We're at the heart of the Devon Moors.

TANYA: Yes, exactly, trapped.

OLIVER: Can I show it to you, the room?

MAKSIM (*To TANYA.*): He's asking to take us down now.

TANYA: ...and what, rob and kill us?

OLIVER: What about something to drink?

MAKSIM: It's something we never got at Winter's.

TANYA looks from one to the other.

Lighting shift.

The sound of doors slamming in regular succession accompanies MAKSIM and TANYA moving in. The light intensifies on the room, where 'MISS HIGHLIGHTS' is seen. This boy is androgynous rather than camp. He flinches when FRANKLYN speaks.

MAKSIM: We could save as much as £10,000 and then go to Canada.

TANYA: As long as we don't get deported.

MAKSIM: I'm referring to when we're deported, say, in two years' time. Trust me, these things take that long.

FRANKLYN (Mock chanting, off.): Bless and keep us, Miss Highlights. Miss H lets her countenance shine upon us and give us peace. Blessed be the name of Miss H!

TANYA: Alcoholics are living here, too?

MAKSIM (Crossing to the 'door'.): I don't know how many others.

TANYA: Other women would be nice.

MAKSIM looks out. MISS HIGHLIGHTS signals him from inside the room.

MISS HIGH: Don't provoke him.

MAKSIM: Huh? Who?

MISS HIGH: Franklyn Gerontius – Oliver's nephew. Are you the new ones? We need to become acquainted.

MAKSIM (Squinting.): Where are you?

MISS HIGH (Into the light.): In here.

FRANKLYN: I have a feel-ing...you're not alone!

MISS HIGH: Can you come inside if you're coming? He'll attack if he sees you.

MAKSIM: We're trying to find our room.

MISS HIGH: Yes, in here. (Crossing to them.) He's come back from the pub in the village. (Moving MAKSIM inside.) ...and he's wild.

They are 'in the room'.

MAKSIM: Tanyush?

TANYA: We've got to get to bed...if we start work at seven.

MISS HIGH: I work in the kitchen...my name's Dorian. But he calls me something provocative. Don't ask me to tell you what. It's based on the fact that I colour my hair, though. I detest him.

MAKSIM: How many others are working here?

TANYA: Maksim.

MAKSIM: Wait a minute. *(To MISS HIGHLIGHTS.)* Any other women on the staff?

MISS HIGH: You're not frightened of us, are you?

MAKSIM: I was thinking of my wife.

MISS HIGH *(To TANYA.)*: Oh, yes, hello. I can see what you mean. Well, let's see. We did have a Japanese girl...Yuni. Then there's Georgina, looking after the rooms. I think you'll be working with...Why are you looking so oddly at me? *(To MAKSIM.)* Please tell her to stop it.

MAKSIM: She doesn't speak English.

MISS HIGH: Yes, well, I'm asking you. I can't help how I look.

MAKSIM: Her problem is she doesn't understand. *(To TANYA.)* He thinks you're being rude.

TANYA: I'm just trying to get him to leave.

MAKSIM *(To MISS HIGHLIGHTS.)*: She means nothing by it.

TANYA *(To MISS HIGHLIGHTS.)*: You...go...away!

MAKSIM: He says there's another girl...working with you.

TANYA: I don't give a fuck – get him out of here.

MISS HIGH: What's that, Russian you're speaking?

MAKSIM: We're very tired, if you wouldn't mind...

MISS HIGH: I am, myself. So let me tell you about the sleeping arrangements. The sofa lets out into a bed.

MAKSIM: We'll discover all that for ourselves.

MISS HIGH: No, you see, it's going to be my bed...where I sleep. Unless you have other ideas.

MAKSIM: But this is our room.

MISS HIGH: Yes...and the bedroom. And mine. Though I understand, you want privacy.

MAKSIM: We want this room to ourselves!

TANYA: What's going on here? Isn't this ours?

MAKSIM (To TANYA.): Just a minute here.

MISS HIGH: Well, where am I going to sleep? Franklyn's liable to do anything after his drinking...and to me especially...you don't know what he's capable of.

MAKSIM: That's nothing to do with us.

MISS HIGH: It has to be if you're staying here – you can't escape it.

MAKSIM (Starting out.): I'm going to go see the manager.

MISS HIGH: Oliver? He's the owner, and he'll be asleep.

TANYA: Where are you going? Don't leave me with him.

MAKSIM: I'll only be a minute.

MISS HIGH: I warned you, remember. About Franklyn, too. Please don't tell him I'm here.

FRANKLYN (Shadowy.): You enjoy coming out, don't you, Dor-ian? Miss Highlights? So why are you hiding from me?

MISS HIGH: Don't go out yet, I beg you.

TANYA: This is crazy. Let's get out of here. You hear me, Maksim? Telephone a taxi, back to the station. Winter's Rest is far better than this. (To MISS HIGHLIGHTS.) You must go. We must to sleep. Go. Go. To sleep.

MISS HIGH: If only I could, love.

MAKSIM has been on his mobile.

MAKSIM: Mr... (*Looking at MISS HIGHLIGHTS.*)

MISS HIGH: ...Oliver.

MAKSIM: There seems to be a confusion, can you come down? (*A beat.*) Maksim Pavlov.... (*A beat.*) All right, but I tell you, we can't stay under these conditions. (*A beat.*) I'm sorry.

MISS HIGH: Sorry about what? You never got him to come down?

TANYA: What the fuck's happening?

OLIVER appears out of the shadows.

OLIVER: I never gave it another thought, to be honest. Aren't you Russkies used to communal living?

MAKSIM: You didn't know we were Russian when I rang up.

OLIVER: I'd no idea there'd be two of you. Dorrie used to share with a boy named Jan. Call it foolish, but I assumed you'd be more like him...Well, alone, anyway.

MAKSIM: But I told you on the phone there were two of us.

OLIVER: I know you did – it slipped my mind. I must have been thinking about something else. Or I thought about what I expected to happen. Have you ever experienced that?

MAKSIM: Are you going to suggest a solution? We want to get quickly to bed.

OLIVER: Well, now, Georgina's room is just down the hall. They'll be working together – why don't she and Tanya share?

MAKSIM: Because Tanya and I are married. Do you understand?

OLIVER: I'm familiar with the practice. There's no need to be rude.

MAKSIM: Two men and a woman can't live together. Can't you see?

OLIVER: For the sake of the sofa, I'm sure Dorrie wouldn't mind my saying – he's hardly a –

MAKSIM: I don't care what he is, we're not going to stay here if he does.

OLIVER: All right. I'll sort something out by the morning.

MAKSIM: My wife wants it sorted out now.

OLIVER: Quite a terrier, is she? Is it all right he leaves his things tonight?

MISS HIGH: Are you asking me to leave?

OLIVER: The Russians are doing the asking.

MISS HIGH: But you agree to it? I'm afraid to go out that door.

OLIVER: Nonsense, I'm going out with you.

MISS HIGH: Franklyn's back...he'll see where we've gone.

OLIVER: Is that so difficult?

MISS HIGH: Your nephew, I'm sorry to say, is very strange. You must know of his attitude toward me.

OLIVER: But it's not personal, dear. He's a drinker, and drinkers, you know, hate the world. I hope that doesn't sound sanctimonious, when hospitality's our metier...

MAKSIM: Excuse me, please.

TANYA: You want me to do it myself?

Lighting shift.

FRANKLYN comes out of the shadow, with a bottle or two in tow.

FRANKLYN: Don't think I'm intruding – I just brought you these.

MAKSIM (*Trying to move him out.*): And then you're leaving?

FRANKLYN: Sorry?

MAKSIM: We've been working since dawn.

FRANKLYN: There's the weekend ahead.

MAKSIM: Yeah, we're working then, too, double shift.

TANYA is slightly groggy from trying to rest.

TANYA: No..no...He brought us drink? Let him stay. (To FRANKLYN.) Spasobichki. Sank you very much.

FRANKLYN (Moving in.): You know what they say about wetting the baby's head? Well, I wet the weekend ahead...even when it's Tuesday. You got any glasses?

TANYA (Up on her feet with alacrity.): No, no...I do. You zits down.

MAKSIM (Correcting her.): 'Sit' down.

TANYA: 'Zit.'

MAKSIM: 'Sit'...Try saying it with 'ts'.

FRANKLYN: Try shutting up about it...What does it matter? I'm with the wogs in this – I sits where I pisses.

MAKSIM: She has to start learning good English.

FRANKLYN: Yeah, but you know what, for your guests? It's bloody boring.

A pause. TANYA, gingerly, gives FRANKLYN a glass.

MAKSIM: You work...is that right...in the kitchen?

FRANKLYN: So you got Wanda Wonderbra out of here? (Lifts his glass.) To you! (To TANYA.) Spastic – whatever. Like to cut out its heart...fry it up in a mixed grill including its goolies. He'd probably be grateful for that. And I don't want him anywhere near me.

MAKSIM: In Russia, until very recently, people like him were thought criminal.

FRANKLYN: Wait a minute. What do you know about Russia?

MAKSIM: We're Russian.

FRANKLYN: Oh, yeah, like I believe that. You believe I'm related to Fu Manchu? (Slants his eyes.)

MAKSIM: If you said you were, why not?

FRANKLYN: You're fucking whacked. Ought to cut out your heart and all.

TANYA (Hushed.): I don't think he's very nice.

MAKSIM: Yeah, all right.

FRANKLYN: What language is that, Serbo-Croat? *(Laughs.)* So when, exactly, were you in the joint?

MAKSIM: I'm sorry?

FRANKLYN: I thought you said you knew creatures like Ladybird here back in prison.

MAKSIM: I think you misunderstood.

FRANKLYN: I think you're some kind of Porky-pier. If he turned up in any of the places I've been in, he'd be brown bread after the first day. *(Looks at him.)* Oh, Jeez, are you thick or what? Dead, you know? Ker-plunk. Pasted.

MAKSIM: I think that's what I was saying.

FRANKLYN: You never said that at all. What do you take me for?

TANYA: Just leave him alone.

FRANKLYN: What's she saying about me now? *(To TANYA.)* Making jokes about my equipment, were you? *(Hands to his flies.)* I got to prove you wrong?

MAKSIM: She asks...can you leave us alone...please?

FRANKLYN *(In his face.)*: Please...Who wants to fuck with you anyway? *(Gets up to leave. Without the bottles.)* It's bloody bor-ing.

Lighting shift.

TANYA and MAKSIM cross to meet INNA. In the course of the scene – taking place in a pub – OLIVER comes out of the shadows to talk to MAKSIM – presumably back at the hotel. The scenes should dovetail. The first starts with TANYA trying to get INNA to have another drink.

INNA: No, please, no more for me.

TANYA: Really, it's all right...because we work here, you see?

MAKSIM: This bar is attached to the hotel.

TANYA: 'One get...one free'.

INNA *(Giggles.)*: 'One get...one free'...

While they're pouring another round of drinks, for INNA as well – doubles.

MAKSIM: It's actually, 'Buy one...get one free'.

INNA *(Not hearing him.)*: I'm so embarrassed to go out of the shop with 25 packets of Kit Kat...five tubs margarine

TANYA: We have to take what we can get in this job.

MAKSIM: It's not that bad.

TANYA: It's only because the boss fancies you. *(To INNA.)* It's true, you know. Every one in the place is some kind of blue boy.

INNA: It's all over England.

TANYA: I'm beginning to think you're right.

INNA: On the television, late last night, there was a programme like a training course...They were out in the park, you know, hunting, like wolves. *(Pulls a predatory face.)* And then the camera followed them into the public convenience...my God. It was awful...and so funny, believe me. One of them... *(Laughs.)* ....put his hose in a hole...and another one, in the booth next him, takes the hose and he...I-don't-know-what, you know? And there it was, right there, on the television. England, believe me, strange country.

TANYA: Where was Roy while you watched this? Was Celestine there?

MAKSIM: Inna's not there any more. Don't you remember?

TANYA *(to INNA)*: You never told us.

INNA: I married.

TANYA: Inna!

MAKSIM: Yes, I knew.

TANYA looks from one to the other.

MAKSIM: I told you she was moving out.

INNA: I told you myself, one week after you rang me you'd found the job here.

TANYA: Well, yes, of course I remember that part. I thought you...I was getting ready to ask if you wanted a job here. We could both do with the company, and I'm sure Oliver wouldn't mind. He'll do whatever Maksim wants, very nearly. That's the reason we're here.

INNA: I can't work. I'm no longer after asylum.

TANYA: What do you mean? We can't work. *(To MAKSIM.)* Get him over here. She can start this week.

INNA: No, you don't understand. Explain it, Maksim.

TANYA: You can explain it. I'll follow.

INNA: According to English law –

MAKSIM: You and I aren't after anything, except money.

TANYA *(waving him away)*: I know that much. *(To INNA.)* According to law, what?

INNA: If I apply as the wife of an English man –

TANYA: He is English, your husband?

INNA: Yes, he is...and disabled, in fact.

TANYA: Well, what does that have to do with anything?

INNA: It had to do with a lot, once I got into Court. Home Office said I married the only one I could find.

TANYA: Well, that's true, isn't it?

INNA: But I never did anything like Beznik or Abdullah. Finding a girl in a pub, sleeping with her, and saying they're going to get married the next day.

MAKSIM: You don't drink, for a start.

TANYA: Fine, but who's going to know that?

INNA: Anyway, while they're deciding my case, I can't work.

TANYA: But if he's disabled, neither does he. So you're both homeless.

INNA: No, it's not like it is back in Russia...thank you, God.

OLIVER (*loudly, emerging out of the shadows*): And if you'd had faith in me from the start....

Something of a transition. TANYA and INNA recede in shadow while OLIVER takes MAKSIM into the spotlight.

OLIVER: I understand it's been difficult for you.

MAKSIM: Your nephew's mad...dangerous.

OLIVER: But he doesn't work here.

MAKSIM: He lives here.

OLIVER: Not all the time.

MAKSIM: ...a criminal record and Tanya's plain frightened. And who can protect her from that?

OLIVER: Police can...the laws of this country. There's a restraining order forbidding him any contact with ordinary folk. I wouldn't be surprised if he was already on remand. Maybe goes back at the weekends.

MAKSIM: Your business, not ours.

OLIVER: Well, it's not really – how can it be – my...

MAKSIM: It's not meant to be mine and Tanya's – that's what I'm trying to tell you.

OLIVER: Don't you like it with me?

MAKSIM: What do you mean...?

OLIVER: The money I give you, it's not enough?

MAKSIM: Tanya's been working twelve hours sometimes.

OLIVER: I'm glad we're talking about this.

A pause.

You know, now that Christmas is coming...

MAKSIM: What, you want us to work even more?

OLIVER: You're not giving me a chance. Now admit it. You ask for my help, yet you won't hear what I have to offer. Does that even make sense? No, it doesn't. Admit it.

MAKSIM: What is it you want?

OLIVER: We've received several compliments about you from the guests. We must treat you as featured attractions, it seems. And I know why they say it. You're like a pair of walking...what are they called...Russian dolls?

MAKSIM: Matrioshki?

OLIVER: Yes, exactly, that's right.

MAKSIM: And then at Christmas, Father Christmas appears with the Snow Queen...each other's costume.

OLIVER: Well, now, isn't that fun. It chimes perfectly, in fact, with what I had in mind. Would you consider showing us?

MAKSIM: Well, no, the costumes are back home in Russia.

OLIVER: Oh, really? I had in mind, anyway, a sort of family gathering...minus Franklyn, you may be sure. But we'd be on our own, with maybe one or two welcome additions...

MAKSIM: You're giving us the time off?

OLIVER: Oh, yes, as much as you want...afterwards.

MAKSIM: 'After'?

OLIVER: It's the slack time, January. And doesn't that anyway coincide? Don't Russians celebrate later than we do? It's perfect timing, in fact.

MAKSIM: And you could guarantee us...what? How much extra?

OLIVER: So you'll do it then...

TANYA (*Long and plaintively.*): No-oh-oh!

A mini shift has TANYA arguing with MAKSIM. Party laughter is heard, off. Toward the end of their discussion, the lights rise on 'a bedroom' where BRANGWEN is laughing to the brink of her control.

MAKSIM: Hasn't he always paid what he promised?

TANYA: And I want some fucking time off. You hear that – fucking? I'm serious.

MAKSIM: I never thought you weren't. I told Oliver –

TANYA: 'You told Oliver' – what? Your wife wants him to lay off her husband? Did you? He should hire Inna to work with your overworked wife.

MAKSIM: That's up to Inna.

TANYA: He can make her an offer, can't he? To satisfy me? Doesn't' he think I want some laughter?

MAKSIM: That's what I thought he was offering us.

TANYA: In other words, no, I'm his servant to swab out his messes. That's very nice. (*Trailing off.*) The stuff my doll's dreams are about. Fuck him into an early grave.

She tosses a glass down in anger, and this coincides with a bottle breaking in BRANGWEN'S area, bringing a shift in lighting. BRANGWEN addresses someone momentarily out of view.

BRANGWEN (*Happily*): We'll have to pay extra for that, you know. To say nothing of other replacements. And then it's Christmastime. What if they run out? I hope this isn't a sample of our married life to come.

TANYA comes on with cleaning material. They don't recognize each other for the moment.

TANYA: Something's break here?

BRANGWEN: Well, yes, we're sorry. A bottle...

TANYA: Bottle. All bottle. Champagne.

BRANGWEN: Well, yes, I know, it's a frightful waste.

TANYA: Fucking...mess.

BRANGWEN: I...pardon? I can't believe what I just heard. Were you swearing at me?

TANYA: I must pay...fucking mess. Clean up. After pay.

BRANGWEN: That's not really the –

TANYA: ...fucking.

BRANGWEN: Stop saying that to me.

A pause. TANYA begins to clean up. BRANGWEN is tearful.

I suppose it doesn't matter to you at all you've completely spoiled my honeymoon. This dream of a holiday hotel...for which we've paid an undisclosed fortune has now turned into a nightmare for us. And very much you care. Yes, thank you, very much.

BEZNIK now comes into view and immediately recognizes TANYA.

BEZNIK: Darling Tanya. Khalo!

TANYA: What are you talking about?

BRANGWEN: Why are you calling...why 'darling'? This woman used language to me.

BEZNIK: You don't know...little Tanya?

BRANGWEN: Well, I never thought...

BEZNIK: Brangwen and me...married now.

BRANGWEN: ...and are you working here? you and...erm.

BEZNIK: Wonder...yes...we drink champagne!

TANYA: You could if it wasn't all over the floor...for me to clean up. And how did you happen to come here anyway? Of all places?

BRANGWEN: It's probably my own inner failing. But you know I can't understand a syllable of what you're saying.

TANYA: Did you tail after Inna, is that how you did it?

BEZNIK: Inna? Inna marry, too...American English man. To America, bye-bye.

TANYA: Did the Home Office offer you money for turning us in? Passport?

BEZNIK: Passport? I get passport, sure.

BRANGWEN: I'm sure it would be lovely to stay here and natter, if we only spoke each other's... It's hard enough knowing what he says.

TANYA: I just want to tell you...it won't work. *(Trying to speak English.)* Okay? Fucking off.

BRANGWEN *(Tearful.)*: That's the language she used in the first place! And she can't tell me what I did wrong.

Dovetailing into this scene, the lights come up sharply on FRANKLYN smashing the glass of the fire extinguisher.

BEZNIK: Fucking hell.

BRANGWEN: Does that mean we're now on fire!

OLIVER challenges FRANKLYN.

OLIVER: Are you completely out of your senses?

FRANKLYN *(Axe in hand.)*: I'm warning you, coz. Stay back.

OLIVER: I suppose it's utterly slipped your notice or concern that you've also triggered the police alarm.

Doors heard opening.

There's no need whatever to panic. Believe me. It's a false alarm! Somebody's seasonal prank... out of hand. Happy hols one and all. *(Back to FRANKLYN.)* They're going to be here any minute, don't worry.

FRANKLYN: Fucking...animal.

OLIVER: That's it, yes. Run for your life. *(He's referring to the fact that FRANKLYN himself looks like a hunted animal. He lets out a primal scream as he runs off.)*

VOICE: Is somebody going to shut that damn thing off?

OLIVER: I've just had a thought about something else. There is no need to panic. But regulations, I'm afraid. We'll all have to vacate the building. I do apologize.

At another part of the stage, MAKSIM and TANYA find each other.

MAKSIM: Are you all right?

TANYA: Depends what you mean by –

MAKSIM: But you're not hurt or anything. And there's no fire?

TANYA: There's a mess in the bedroom. Are you sure there isn't?

MAKSIM: Only that lunatic Franklyn...and they know it. It's nothing to do with me this time.

TANYA: We're still going to have to leave.

MAKSIM: I've sorted it out.

TANYA: I said 'had to', you idiot. Our cover's blown. The Home Office are onto us.

MAKSIM: My God...was it Inna.

TANYA: No, of course it wasn't Inna, my idiot darling.

The fire alarm stops.

MAKSIM: My God. Who?

Instant fade.

ACT TWO

Scotland.

MAKSIM and TANYA face each other centre stage as though they are about to dance. Down centre facing the audience, hotel manager McBrodie speaks, heavily accented.

McBRODIE: I've already told you I like what you have to offer. On that I trust we've no argument. It's your wee wife we're concerned with exclusively. If she'll no learn English, how can you continue to work together? I mean, you...well, the ceiling's the limit, as far goes the hotel trade. And I'll give it to you – she'd be a positive peach in reception. Without the language, however? Can you honestly see her in anathing other than cleaning up? She couldna even wait table. Best advised she attend evening classes.

TANYA: Scotland's wonderful.

MAKSIM: We're going to take breathtaking trips.

TANYA: Without worrying about closing hours.

MAKSIM: He told you to take an evening class.

TANYA: That won't interfere with my drinking.

McBRODIE (Approaching him.): You take, for example, a professional-amateur golf tournament. Organizers have offered this as the main catering venue. What if I was to arrange it that you'd be in overall charge? I don't want to hear that your wife has qualms. Her opinion hasn't been sought. You see what I'm saying to you. Every man in the room has a wife which he talks to in exactly the same way. It's understood.

TANYA (An English-lesson-sentence, heavily accented.): I have my bread in the hope that it does not fall butter-side down. This is what is known as a homily.

She takes a drink. NATALYA taps her on the shoulder. McBRODIE stands over her.

NATALYA: Excuse me, please. You work at the hotel? You are Russian?

TANYA (Looks at her.): You're a guest?

NATALYA (Warmly.): I work there, too, from today. (Holding her hand out.) Natalya Rospova... Tasha. What's the matter?

McBRODIE (*Overlapping.*): The verb 'to conjugate' is the one you must treat as the key. It does not mean sleep with your boyfriend, rather, 'Which tense must I use when?' and how. That is its true definition. All right?

TANYA, meanwhile, has attempted to walk past NATALYA.

NATALYA: I'm sure you're the right girl. I've seen you there talking with somebody else...Is that your husband?

McBRODIE: Example: the auxiliary verb 'must', auxiliary meaning, 'to help'. One verb helping another, like one person helping another.

TANYA (*Cod 'English' to NATALYA.*): I must to learn the English.

McBRODIE: Exactly. 'I must do what I'm paid for', precise meaning, 'I have no choice.' Got the idea? 'Must' is essential vocab for you...more important than 'Give me a drink.' 'Give me money.' You must, before you can get, work. 'Get one free' doesn't work...at least for me.

NATALYA: Why are you being so difficult?

TANYA: Can you speak it? If we spend all our time together, we'll both get sacked.

NATALYA: I don't know anybody else.

TANYA: Then you'll learn that much quicker than I do.

McBRODIE now approaches NATALYA.

McBRODIE (*Slowly.*): Do you know any English language?

NATALYA: I try...try to learn...to study.

McBRODIE: That's a good girl. And are you going to college? Classes? In the evening?

NATALYA: Night?

McBRODIE: The night time is only for study and sleep. Never ever for drinking and...other things.

MAKSIM approaches TANYA.

MAKSIM: If you tried hard, I think you could work waiting tables. There's a restaurant attached. I think you'd better. I had to turn him down.

TANYA: Why? What do you mean?

MAKSIM: The conference he wanted me to work at would have meant leaving you. And I told him no. So I think he'll be watching us closely from now on.

TANYA is a bit groggy.

Can you at least try to get out of bed?

McBRODIE: There's an opening for someone with your kind of promise. I had hopes for another girl, but I've been let down.

NATALYA smiles obligingly without really comprehending.

TANYA: Couldn't we go somewhere else...if he let us go?

MAKSIM: You said you liked Scotland so much.

TANYA: Somewhere else in Scotland.

MAKSIM: Wouldn't we have the same problems? You can't speak.

NATALYA (To McBRODIE.): I want to learn...all I can.

McBRODIE: And I want to help you, my dear. Okay, that's splendid.

MAKSIM tries to rouse TANYA.

MAKSIM: How much did you have to drink?

TANYA: It's not fair. You never have anything like the amount that I do, so you're always all right. And you speak English. You see? It's just not fair.

MAKSIM: So you're saying it's my fault for speaking English?

TANYA: It's plainly my fault that I don't.

MAKSIM: We couldn't have come here if I hadn't.

TANYA: Exactly. You did it to suit yourself.

McBRODIE and NATALYA separate. He crosses to talk to MAKSIM, she crosses over to TANYA.

TANYA: No, you go off to the conference – what's stopping you? I'll go alone to the pub.

MAKSIM: You're going to have more to drink?

TANYA: ...after cleaning the fucking loos, sure, why not?

McBRODIE (To MAKSIM.): I'm afeared I need this quiet word with you.

MAKSIM: ...about working the conference, yes? I'm available for it.

McBRODIE: You may be available, but I've had to look elsewhere, I'm sorry. And someone's had a word in my ear you've borrowed one of our space heaters. Now when I said you were hotel material, I didna expect you'd be taking it all for granted.

MAKSIM: The heater's mine... Do you want me to show the receipt?

McBRODIE: I'm everything you could want for an employer, but –

MAKSIM: The heater's mine!

McBRODIE: You're not serious.

MAKSIM: I bought it from Curry's two weeks ago. (Showing receipt.)

McBRODIE (After looking at it.): Someone's engaging in tittle-tattle.

MAKSIM: Who?

McBRODIE: Ah, no. There's no room in the hotel for secret vendettas. We'll draw a line under this like we've forgotten your mistake with the sporting tournament.

MAKSIM: What do you mean my mistake?

McBRODIE: I tell you it's forgotten.

MAKSIM: But I never knew you were ordering me!

McBRODIE: You're a clever boy. I've already told you. Only you want to make sure you don't miss your chance. Like arguing with your employers whenever the fancy takes you. Or letting the envious ones hold you back.

MAKSIM: I don't think I know what you mean.

McBRODIE: Course you do – you're a clever macelvoy. And fond of you as I am, I cannot afford to make a place for that wife of yours merely because she's your wife. Who are you, when the dust settles? And who the hell-and-gone is she? One look and the world knows you married beneath yourself. That may be your business, but you offered me something different in a worker. Something better. You'll no tell me I'm wrong about this.

MAKSIM: She works the same hours I do.

McBRODIE: Doing what? I've got her cleaning the toilets because she's your wife. But I have to be honest with you – we've our own untrained lassies for that kind of work. And you led me to think I'd be buying a pair.

MAKSIM: Tanya's family is starving in the Ukraine.

McBRODIE: That cannot concern me for its own sake. Someone's told me she's fond of her tipple.

MAKSIM: What does that mean? My knowledge of English does not include jargon.

McBRODIE: I'm trying to tell you she's not good enough. (A beat.) With a higher position, you could afford to keep her at home.

MAKSIM: At home where? We'll lose the room here if we don't both have jobs. (McBRODIE sighs.) How much longer can you keep her on? Do you want me to train her? What do you want her to do...and when? For God's sake, speak.

Overlapping.

TANYA appears with a bucket and mop, busy 'cleaning the toilet'. NATALYA coughs.

NATALYA: The manager seems very friendly to me. Is he that way to you?

TANYA (After a beat.): No. He's a swine.

NATALYA: Is that because you don't know English very well? He tried teaching me English, I think.

TANYA: He wants your bottom.

NATALYA: My bottom? For hard work? I think he wants me to work very hard.

TANYA: He wants sex.

NATALYA: That's...not possible, is it?

TANYA: That's up to you.

NATALYA: No, I mean –

TANYA: It's not possible with me – I'm married. And he knows it. So I'm cleaning his toilets. Give him your arse – for sex – and maybe you'll get a bouquet. If you don't, I'll probably fight you for this job. (Making an appropriate sound.) What a prospect.

NATALYA: You see, I came alone...Yaroslavl.

TANYA: I couldn't give a damn.

NATALYA: My mother left us – my brother and me – for a whole summer when I was twelve. Daniel was nine. Our father left us for good just after I was born...my mother says. That's why she needs to go out and find work. And there was nothing in our flat for those three months but dried pasta and tea. And I haven't been able to eat pasta since.

TANYA: If you're twelve, open up. Let me see your baby teeth.

NATALYA: You haven't been listen –

TANYA: That's right. And if you're only twelve, then you're too young to be working here. Don't look to me to mother you.

NATALYA: She came back...by the end of the summer!

TANYA: There's no fluff on you, that's for damn certain.

NATALYA: What, you think I should feel ashamed? What for? We're two women trying to have a conversation.

TANYA: I am one woman trying to clean out the shit from this bowl...because my parents haven't had light for two years.

NATALYA: Haven't had light? Why? Are they blind? I'm so –

TANYA: No, Natalya Only-Pasta-For-Three-Months. They've been without electricity.

NATALYA: That's not poss –

TANYA: I don't give a damn.

NATALYA: But where in Russia is anything that bad?

TANYA: Outer Siberia. *(A beat.)* They're in the Ukraine.

NATALYA: My brother's become alcoholic.

TANYA: My dog has fleas. My brother skins dogs for a living. Eats the flesh, sells the fur. The neighbours below on the balcony shout, 'Hey, Sos! The dogs are dripping fat...and they stink.'

NATALYA: He doesn't still stay with your parents, does he?

TANYA: God...She must be twelve. We've all had a hard time in Russia – that's why we left. The older the person, the harder the circumstance, in a way. There's been more to overcome. I don't want to know you as friend. I'm not lonely...I'm not especially kind.

NATALYA: Someone said you're a nurse.

TANYA: Someone said it. Not someone. My magpie husband. So you've met him. How thrilling for you. *(A beat.)* You want some vodka...all right?

NATALYA: No, I told you – my brother's an alcoholic. *(Suddenly she starts to stumble and cough.)*

TANYA: I'm not so sure that you're not.

McBRODIE now separates from MAKSIM.

NATALYA: I sometimes...well, lately I've been having dizzy spells. But not from drink. Oh, no. We learned not to have it in the house. *(A beat.)* I've always been worried it was my fault...the poor care I took of Dan when –

TANYA: Christ in Heaven, no more of your stories.

McBRODIE *(Calling back.)*: I'll be ready with another log on the fire!

NATALYA: He wouldn't really want me for –

TANYA: How on earth would I know?

NATALYA *(Calling after him; heavily accented.)*: Mr McBrodie!

TANYA: Good God. She's gone to find out.

NATALYA'S gone after McBRODIE. MAKSIM moves to join TANYA, who 'finishes up'. Their scene together lapses into a local pub. ARABELLA, a local, hovers.

MAKSIM: Hallo.

TANYA greets this much as she greeted NATALYA'S overture – preoccupied with work.

TANYA: Have you gone and come back or not bothered to go?

MAKSIM: He asked someone else, in the end.

TANYA: You can't blame me for that!

MAKSIM: I'm not going to.

TANYA: You owe me a drink for it, in fact. I just about ordered you to go. So staying was your decision.

MAKSIM: I said it was. Let's go without talking about it.

This is probably the shift to the pub.

TANYA: Another Russian's now working at the hotel.

MAKSIM: I know – McBrodie told me.

TANYA: But you don't know who it is.

MAKSIM: Is she all right? *(He pours her a drink.)*

TANYA: What do you mean? You think I met her? Exchanged Moscow addresses...swapped anecdotes?

MAKSIM: There must have been something between you. McBrodie couldn't have told you, too.

TANYA: And when did you meet? She said you'd been talking together.

MAKSIM: She didn't tell you? Then it couldn't have been very good.

TANYA: Let's stop this, all right? I'm not jealous, if that's what you mean. I think she's young, silly, she's nothing in common with us, and I'm going to steer clear. Please get me another drink.

MAKSIM: You're drinking too quickly.

TANYA: And she made me think too much about home.

MAKSIM rises to fetch more drink. ARABELLA seizes her chance. Unless otherwise noted, TANYA is assumed to be speaking Russian.

ARABELLA: Men are such boors when you need them to be something else. *(Sitting.)* They force you to take extreme and unladylike measures.

TANYA *(Deadpan.)*: My husband's coming right back.

ARABELLA: Is that Russian you're speaking? Dosvidaniya is about all I know.

TANYA: That's just what I want to say to you – goodbye.

ARABELLA: Oh, right. That's how you pronounce it. *(Rising.)* If I got us both White Russians, d'ye reckon we'd begin to forget our unfortunate histories? The unfortunate parts of our pasts?

TANYA: She's actually taking off!

ARABELLA has gone only as far as the table to get her own drink.

ARABELLA *(Sitting down.)*: We'll make it the next round – I see we're both plentifully supplied. *(Looking at her.)* You're an angel in miniature, aren't you? You're exquisite. You must have been told that before.

TANYA *(Now in English.)*: My husband...come back...quickly. Husband...Man.

ARABELLA: And then you're so soft to the touch. *(Begins running her fingers over TANYA's face.)*

TANYA: Stop.

ARABELLA: You mean it's exciting you? It is me...I don't mind admitting. I wish I knew the Russian for 'turned on'. *(More emphatically.)* The word for 'beautiful' ... you?

MAKSIM returns.

MAKSIM: Excuse me, we're together.

ARABELLA *(Trying it on.)*: I don't think so, McTavish – she and I are. Find yourself something to fiddle with.

TANYA (*Beseechingly.*): What's she trying to do?

MAKSIM: Why are you so surprised? You called it the English Disease.

TANYA: Here in Scotland?

ARABELLA: Hey...hey. Would you mind not talking beyond me? It's indescribably rude.

MAKSIM: We're married...all right? Now why don't you leave us alone?

ARABELLA: Does your brother think you're not entitled to any fun of your own? (*To MAKSIM.*) I'll wager you've no idea how hard this woman works.

MAKSIM: And you'd be precisely and utterly wrong.

ARABELLA: 'Precisely and utterly', is it? I say she's a poppet. (*To TANYA.*) And you want to come home with me.

TANYA: At least make her stop touching me.

MAKSIM (*Standing up, taking ARABELLA'S hand away.*): She doesn't want you to touch her.

ARABELLA: I bet I could make you care. (*A beat.*) Can't we even exchange mobile numbers? Come on.

TANYA: I can't believe this just happened to me.

MAKSIM: Yeah, whatever you do, don't smile.

He begins to lead TANYA away. ARABELLA tries to follow, calling after them.

ARABELLA: My name really is Arabella! I love you! Hey...hey, Golden Balls. I bet she doesn't give it to you tonight!

Lighting shift.

As they move back 'to the hotel', NATALYA is featured stumbling and coughing, out of their view. During their next exchange, she makes her way 'to the toilet'.

TANYA: I don't know what's wrong with this country. (*Leans on MAKSIM for support.*) 'Great Britain'. Sexual maniacs. After you down there so we have to go here. And here they go after me.

MAKSIM: It might not have happened if...

TANYA: What 'might'? I can understand men...you know. There's Beznik. But her...? And those maniacs that were after you. Oliver...and 'Miss...' What was her name?

MAKSIM: His...Are you all right?

TANYA: Yes, I'm all right. I'm something like angry...Sad...for her.

MAKSIM: Sad for who – Natalya?

TANYA: 'Who?' That woman just now. Who's Natalya?

MAKSIM: From Yaroslavl.

TANYA: Oh. (A beat.) She told you where she was from? You chatted that much? She's a magpie like you.

MAKSIM: She lived with her mother and –

TANYA: Yeah, don't bother. She also told me.

NATALYA is heard throwing up.

There she is now. My God. Whatever you say about me, I'm not that bad.

MAKSIM: What, you think that's from drink?

TANYA: She says she doesn't...

MAKSIM: I think she must really be ill. (Crosses to the toilet.) Are you all right...? Natalya?

TANYA (Following him.): That's the one I just finished cleaning.

MAKSIM (Over her.): Shut up. (Back to NATALYA.) Can you speak? Can you open the door?

NATALYA (Struggling.): Who's that?

MAKSIM: Maksim Pavlov. We met this afternoon. (A beat.) Do you know where you are?

NATALYA (A beat.): Is...Tanya with you?

MAKSIM (Somewhat relieved.): Yes, she's here. (Guiding TANYA forward.) Talk to her.

TANYA (*Hushed.*): And what do I say? (*To NATALYA.*) Tasha? It's me. Can you come out? What can we do for you? What's wrong?

MAKSIM: She'll need a doctor.

TANYA: Shut up. (*To NATALYA.*) Tasha, please let us help you. Open the door. (*To MAKSIM.*) She said she suffers from dizziness.

NATALYA comes out of the darkness looking wretched. She needs help in order to stand, and her words are partially indistinct. She's also crying profusely. MAKSIM and TANYA both support her.

NATALYA: ...can't....s-see...c-can't...s-spea. (*Recovering somewhat.*) Tan-tan yush? I'm sorry. I've been sick.

TANYA: What's wrong with you?

MAKSIM: I'm going to phone the Emergencies. (*As he leaves them.*) Can you manage?

TANYA: Don't leave us. Let's get her to bed first. (*To NATALYA.*) All right?

The trio cross the stage.

NATALYA: You're both...very kind.

TANYA (*Past NATALYA, in hushed voice.*): We're not, you know. I was horrible to her. (*To NATALYA.*) I didn't know you were ill.

NATALYA: I want to sleep...very...

MAKSIM: I'm phoning an ambulance.

TANYA (*To NATALYA.*): No, you shouldn't sleep yet. Maksim is getting you a doctor. Can you stay awake? It's free in this country. Are you still awake? Did we tell you my family's from Zhitomir?

Lighting and scene shift as MAKSIM begins to ring through. Funereal atmosphere as McBRODIE and TANYA stand apart, each delivering a 'eulogy'.

McBRODIE: Nabody toold me, ya see? Here am I expecting to see her at work...she's not there. And next week she's away. I'm beginning to be a wee bit angry, thinking she's done a runner. She did, too, it turns out. The ultimate runner, aye.

TANYA: And what I tell her? 'We've all had it harder than you'. Shows what I know. We're all still alive. Twelve years old – she was trying to tell me. She's like those kids in Beslan. I hope she's meeting them now. I'm sure she likes it.

POLBOI, in black leather, approaches MAKSIM.

POLBOI: Who's it for?

MAKSIM: Russian girl. Natalya. *(Realizes he's speaking to another Russian.)* Hallo?

POLBOI *(Shaking hands.)*: Polboi...Viktor...Vitia.

MAKSIM: Pavlov. *(A beat.)* Are you family?

POLBOI: Let's go for a drink.

MAKSIM: I'm meant to be at work. *(Smiles.)* This isn't Russia.

POLBOI: I'd like to know what happened.

MAKSIM: Well...Damn it, yes, why not? You've come all this distance.

POLBOI: ...and she was alone. Was she?

MAKSIM *(Looking over at TANYA.)*: I'll just get my wife.

POLBOI: Can't we talk about this by ourselves?

MAKSIM: Yes, of course. Only Tanya was with her as well.

POLBOI: I'd feel easier.

MAKSIM *(Trying to catch TANYA's eye.)*: Tanya?

POLBOI *(Booming voice.)*: Tanya!

TANYA sees them.

TANYA: What's happening? *(Starts across.)*

MAKSIM *(Calling.)*: No, no – you stay there. I'm just going...

POLBOI has MAKSIM in a bear hug.

MAKSIM: A relative of Tasha's!

TANYA: I don't think so! Her brother is younger...And she didn't have any other males! Leave him alone.

MAKSIM: I'll be all right!

POLBOI: Worries about you, your missus? That's great.

MAKSIM *(Hurting from his grasp.)*: Where do you want to go?

POLBOI: Are we in private? This is good enough. *(He relaxes his grip and takes out a bottle of vodka.)* You got glasses?

MAKSIM: Once again, it's not like in Russia. Here they have pubs. I'm not sure it isn't actually illegal to drink in the street.

POLBOI: But you said we were private, yeah?

MAKSIM: You're not her brother, are you?

POLBOI: Whose? Oh, that girl's?

MAKSIM: You didn't actually know her, did you? Who are you really?

POLBOI: Don't piss yourself. I knew her. Natalya, right? How'd she die again?

MAKSIM *(A beat.)*: She had a brain tumour.

POLBOI: Shit.

MAKSIM: And she lay in a coma for three days. Tanya and I rushed her in...operated on the next day. Woke up once after surgery...and then –

POLBOI: That's all right, don't tell me any more. *(A beat.)* It's a bitch, isn't it. *(Drinks.)*

MAKSIM: What makes it worse is that we didn't really know her ourselves, except for about three days. She'd just started at the hotel where we work...

POLBOI: And where is that again?

MAKSIM: In this city. *(A beat.)* 'Again'?

POLBOI: Drink up...come on. *(Proffers the bottle.)*

MAKSIM: I don't want any more.

POLBOI: 'Any more'? You haven't had anything yet. Now come on. We got to drink to Natalya. Don't we?

MAKSIM: I've got to get back.

POLBOI: Not really your line of work, is it? *(Gripping his shoulder.)* What are you, a waiter? Boot black? *(Short laugh.)*

MAKSIM: I asked you – who the hell are you?

POLBOI: Just a lawyer...like you.

Somewhere round this point ALENKA approaches TANYA. The two duologues now overlap.

ALENKA: Hallo, Tanya.

TANYA *(Eyes fixed on MAKSIM.)*: Don't disturb me... *(Realizes who she is talking to. Stunned.)* Alenka! *(Moves a step closer.)* Am I dreaming?

ALENKA *(Moving next to her.)*: No, it's me. *(Kisses her.)* See? Care to touch me? *(Trying to guide her hand.)*

TANYA *(Withdrawing her hand.)*: No, I believe you...now. How are you? Are you well? Are you safe?

ALENKA: No, no, don't worry, I'm all right.

TANYA: I'll go get Maksim; he's –

ALENKA: Yeah, I know. Leave him for a bit.

TANYA: So you know who he's talking to? What's it about?

ALENKA: So. How are the two of you – are you well and safe?

TANYA: Well, yeah. We've just been attending a funeral, which isn't very – Russian girl we worked with. Suddenly...you know.

ALENKA *(Distracted.)*: A tragedy then.

TANYA: Yah. *(A beat.)* So what are you doing here? Are you staying? What's happened?

ALENKA: You mean at home in Kaliningrad? Or Moscow?

TANYA: Just...anything. Don't make me fish.

Overlapping.

POLBOI: The fact is I'd like to offer you another job. Better, cleaner. Much better paid.

MAKSIM: I can't go back to Russia.

POLBOI: No, I know that. I'm talking about here.

MAKSIM: In Scotland?

POLBOI: Back in England. Outside London. Surrey – the gold brick belt.

MAKSIM: We're afraid to go back –

POLBOI: Yeah, I know all about that. It's all right. We give you insurance.

MAKSIM: What kind of – ?

POLBOI *(Laughing.)*: Diplomatic immunity!

MAKSIM: If you're a lawyer, can't you do the job?

POLBOI: Uh-uh. The client wants someone with your expertise. In fact, he specifically asked for you. *(Laughs.)* What an accolade, eh? Nobody ever asked for me personally. It'd be a moment in my career, if they did. So I guess this is your moment.

MAKSIM: One of them.

POLBOI: One of them, eh? Bastard. *(Grins.)*

MAKSIM *(A beat.)*: How did you know where to find me?

POLBOI: You're in hiding, eh? It wasn't too difficult. *(Pours a drink.)* We'll toast your success, all right? Then I'll tell you. Okay? *(Raises his glass.)* Success?

MAKSIM: Thanks. *(Drinks.)*

POLBOI: So. (*Pointing.*) You see those two ladies over there? Recognize them?

MAKSIM: Well, my wife and...

POLBOI: ...and...?

MAKSIM: ...my sister.

Overlapping.

ALENKA: I have to tell you this, late as it is. I'm sorry for the way I treated you, Tanya. You've been a good wife to Maksim, I understand and respect that. And it isn't your fault you're in the spot you're both in.

TANYA: What 'spot', exactly?

ALENKA: Well, you know...hiding out...here. If Maksim hadn't done what he did, you'd both be working back home...in your chosen professions. And I'm sure you advised him against it, didn't you. As I did myself.

TANYA: We're supporting my parents in Zhitomir.

ALENKA: Oh, I know. The poverty there is appalling. And the meagre amount you earn here.

TANYA: It's enough. They're very grateful.

ALENKA: All right, but it's nothing like what you could send if you still lived in Kaliningrad. Where we'd all live together. Come on. And it's all Maksim's fault – that we don't, that you have to live doing terrible jobs.

TANYA: Why are you saying this? Now? I asked you – what's going on?

ALENKA: All right. You want to know what they're talking about? We'll ask them.

The quartet come together, up centre.

POLBOI: This is some kind of reunion, I guess.

MAKSIM: And I guess you don't want to leave us.

POLBOI: Oh, it's not allowed. I'm obliged to stay with you at all times.

MAKSIM: It's worse than being in prison then. Thanks, Alenka.

ALENKA: What are you talking about? Nikolka is in prison...

MAKSIM: ...thanks to me.

ALENKA: All right then, yes, thanks to you.

MAKSIM: That's what I mean. (Mockingly.) Poor Nikolka.

ALENKA: We gave you a great job. What'd you have to go sticking your nose into things that were none of your business.

MAKSIM: Because that's what my business was beginning to be, and I didn't like it.

ALENKA: Shit – why do you have to be such a crusader? And married to the Red Cross. You think it does anything else but make trouble?

MAKSIM: His trouble was trouble for me. Didn't he tell you? Okay, make your mind up who to believe. My side, he was all but ordering me to make a hit on the rival ship owner. Who might well have had me marked anyway. I'd have been shot if I'd gone through with it. I always thought he knew that...and wanted to get rid of me.

ALENKA: Rid of you? You were his brother-in-law...knew all his business. You were even responsible for much of it.

MAKSIM: And he sent you here...to remind me.

ALENKA: No.

MAKSIM: I don't believe you...Well, do you believe me? You've made your choice, Lyen. It's obvious.

ALENKA: No, it's not. Even if you don't give a damn about me any more, there's your own circumstances to think of. You care about those or you don't really care about anything. That's why you'll do what he wants. (Referring to POLBOI.)

POLBOI: It's not a difficult job we're asking. Deliver and explain a set of contracts, that's all. What else do lawyers do, after all?

MAKSIM: It's the penalty for not doing it I'm thinking about.

POLBOI: Oh, sure.

MAKSIM: There's security, being a boot black...or washing toilets, what she does. You sleep soundly at night, even when it's freezing cold. (To TANYA.) Tell them...

TANYA: Tell them...what?

MAKSIM: How happy you are. The pubs stay open.

TANYA: Right, there are no closing hours.

MAKSIM: And the toilets are...

TANYA: ...even the British toilets are clean.

MAKSIM: A tulip garden.

TANYA: Well, I wouldn't go that far.

MAKSIM: People use them for making love.

TANYA (*giggling*): Oh, yes, that's true. Apparently. I've never seen it myself. Well, I mean, why should I? Maksim and I have our own room. All right, it's not the same as we had in Kaliningrad. But it's bigger than most rooms in Moscow, and we're well fed.

ALENKA: And these people know your future is limited...that you broke your conditions of entry...once you're found, you'll be sent back. Not to a country of your choosing, but to Russia. They know that. One phone call is all it takes.

MAKSIM: They know it now anyway. As I say, thanks.

POLBOI: Why have you all got long faces? 'One phone call.' One errand is all we want. It's the same as a long weekend break to the Lake District. That's where it is, in fact. Yes. Believe me. Surrey...London...Lake District. The only addresses I know. And after that, your problems are over.

ALENKA: You've got to do more than think about it. But that's my advice, and you've always only gone your own way.

Light fades on POLBOI and ALENKA and leaves MAKSIM and TANYA alone. Two more shadowy figures begin to appear. But for the moment MAKSIM is busy packing and explaining to TANYA why.

MAKSIM: Take the job and life would be over. You've got to help me decide.

TANYA: What? Your sister said you always did only what you wanted.

MAKSIM: And you take her side? She put us here. What does she know? Do you want to go over our past mistakes? Your family needed money.

TANYA: I know.

MAKSIM: What could I make as a Law lecturer? Less than you as a nurse.

TANYA: I know all that. So what? She said you never took my advice; I didn't. I know what you know...that I never gave it. Maksim? What you've done has always been right.

A pause.

MAKSIM: Well, I'm asking for your advice now. (*She nestles close to him. He stops packing.*) We have to go to Canada now, I think, that's certain. The question is how do we do it? Do we assume to take what Polboi asks...maybe even do the job...I don't know. As soon as we seem to have done it, then we get on the first available flight. That's the first – and the logical – option, I think. The other is simply to lean on McBrodie – ask his contacts to shield us out of here, within the week. It's possible, I think. We'd leave from some Highland airstrip. They wouldn't know where it was. He's even got contacts once we land...if we agree to continue to work in hotels...in Nova Scotia, for instance. That wouldn't be bad to begin with, and they probably don't have as many perverts anyway.

TANYA: But...can I tell you what I think?

MAKSIM: That's why I asked.

TANYA: What if they have this place watched? That man and his friends.

MAKSIM: That's what makes me want to go straight for the first option. Why not begin to do what they want? I know things...that they want to know.

D.I. MARTINS comes out of the shadows, calling out MAKSIM'S name as he approaches.

MARTINS: Maksim Pavlov?

MAKSIM: Yes?

MARTINS: Your current employer told me where to find you and...is this your...wife?

MAKSIM (*An echo of the first scene.*): We're married, yes.

MARTINS: And is it correct that you left Winters Asylum Centre to work at the Crestview Hotel outside Chagford?

MAKSIM: You're from the Home Office.

MARTINS: Devon and Cornwall Police. *(Flashes his badge.)*

TANYA *(Under her breath.)*: My God...

MARTINS: I'd like if I may to ask you some questions concerning events that took place there on the evening of 5 December. You were present?

MAKSIM: We both were.

MARTINS: And you both are or were applying for asylum...Application which has subsequently been refused. *(Consulting notebook. Continuing to look down as he speaks.)* We're not concerned with that as such but as I say with what was alleged to have taken place on the evening or the night-time in question.

MAKSIM: You're...not here about our asylum application?

MARTINS: Why? You've violated conditions of entry, is that right? *(Looks at them now.)* You've failed to report to the police ever since you left Winters Asylum Centre.

MAKSIM: We're continuing with our appeal. Our solicitor is –

MARTINS: I'm investigating another matter.

TANYA *(In the silence.)*: Maksim? What's going on?

MAKSIM: Quiet. *(To MARTINS.)* What matter is – ?

MARTINS: Are you acquainted with Franklyn Gerontius, nephew of the owner of the Crest – ?

MAKSIM: Yes, we both are...or were.

MARTINS: You have a clear picture of who I mean.

MAKSIM: Absolutely.

MARTINS: Do you both speak English, by the way? I understand you're Russian?

MAKSIM: I'm a solicitor. Yes, I do. Tanya's English is a little –

TANYA *(To MARTINS.)*: Little...yes...Better.

MARTINS: But you both remember seeing him that night.

MAKSIM: I think so, yes. That was the evening he set off the fire alarm.

MARTINS: You're sure it was him?

MAKSIM: He boasted he'd done it.

MARTINS: And what sort of man was he? Did you have much contact?

MAKSIM: Oh, yes. Not that very evening, but –

MARTINS: So you were aware of his habits.

MAKSIM: No, only when he was at the hotel.

TANYA: Awful man, Franklyn. Awful...dirty...maniac. I hate him.

MARTINS (*After a moment.*): He was found with his throat cut at 2.34 a.m. on 5 December last.

MAKSIM: So you're saying we're under suspicion.

MARTINS: Suspicion of what? I'm saying nothing for the moment. I'm trying to form a picture of who he was.

MAKSIM: Didn't he have a police record?

MARTINS: How do you know that? Did he tell you himself?

MAKSIM: I can't remember. Yes, I'm sure he did. He boasted...as I say. He would boast about many things.

MARTINS: Go on.

MAKSIM: Well, that was his character. He didn't work at the hotel, as you probably know. His uncle, Oliver, kept a room for him.

MARTINS: And how did you happen to know him?

MAKSIM: Well...he'd bother the hotel staff. It was his character, his sport.

TANYA: Tell him how he'd speak to us.

MARTINS: And what about the others?

MAKSIM: What?

MARTINS: Was his behaviour with them the same?

MAKSIM: I don't know what you mean.

TANYA: I am sure he wanted rape me! I keel him...you know?

MAKSIM: Tanya!

TANYA: Why not? It's the truth.

MAKSIM: Because he's saying he was murdered. Now he'll think that we had something to do with it.

A pause.

(To MARTINS.) When Tanya said 'kill', I'm sure she didn't mean...I'm sure you must have heard that before. It means nothing, doesn't it? And when she said rape.

MARTINS: We've already got someone in custody. We're just trying to build up a case.

MAKSIM: Oh, well, of course. (A beat.) You couldn't say who it is?

MARTINS: Of course not.

MAKSIM: Of course not...sorry.

MARTINS: But in fact you saw nothing of Gerontius that evening or night?

MAKSIM: Heard only...shouting and swearing. Yes, that's right.

MARTINS: All right. Thank you very much. (A beat.) Would you be available for further questioning in the event?

MAKSIM: In the event of what?

MARTINS: You could be called as material witnesses. That's all.

MAKSIM: When this case goes to trial?

MARTINS (Starting to go.): Yes, that's right. (Turns back.) I think I can tell you this much. From everything we've been able to piece together, it was a murder made to happen. In other words, he's not likely to be missed. Several people, at least, openly echoed your wife's sentiments. Goodnight.

A pause.

TANYA: Maksim?

MAKSIM: Just a minute.

TANYA: Did I understand? We're not going to be able to leave?

MAKSIM: And all this time...we've been worried about being deported...and the police have known about us...all this time. And, in the end, when they finally catch up with us, they're worried about someone else? An English maniac? Is that how you see it, too?

TANYA: I'm not sure. I didn't really understand what he was saying.

MAKSIM: But about Franklyn – you understood that.

TANYA: Well, he's dead. Yes. Good.

MAKSIM: That's right! You even made what they call 'incriminating statements', and he couldn't have cared less. You were expressing the general opinion!

TANYA: Well, all right...

MAKSIM: No, it's better than that, don't you see? We could stay here forever ... without the asylum. And they wouldn't care!

TANYA: Are we going to do that?

MAKSIM: Well, the pressure is off us at least. (A beat.) Why were you so sure that our cover had been blown?

TANYA: That night? I saw Beznik with Brangwen.

MAKSIM: What do you mean?

TANYA: They were staying there. She said they were married.

MAKSIM: You're crazy.

TANYA: That's what I mean. They'd tracked us down to the hotel, and were waiting to inform on us.

MAKSIM: But even if they did, it didn't matter.

TANYA: Didn't it?

MAKSIM: Of course not. What did he say?

TANYA: You speak English.

MAKSIM: They've known about us from the beginning. And yet...we're still here. (*A beat.*) You want to go for a drink...to celebrate?

TANYA: I don't want to see that crazy girl.

MAKSIM: We'll go somewhere else. Or I'll be with you the whole time. Nobody's going to bother you.

They start out.

TANYA: I keep thinking it would have been nice to take Tasha with us....to have her as a friend.

MAKSIM: You know, I completely forgot about her? It's a shame.

TANYA: It's worse than that. For her, of course. But also for us. We're alone here except for each other. Her friendship would have been –

MAKSIM: That's why I still think Canada's our future.

TANYA: You mean it's possible?

MAKSIM: I think it's essential. You said it exactly. We're alone here except for maniacs, hotel managers...

TANYA: ...dirty toilets.

MAKSIM: It's better than Russia.

TANYA: It's a toilet. What's better about that?

MAKSIM: Canada!

SCOOBY steps out of the shadows.

SCOOBY: Hey, Pavlov!

MAKSIM: What? Are you one of Polboi's goons?

SCOOBY: My name's Scooby.

MAKSIM: If you're also a friend of my sister...

SCOOBY: What?

MAKSIM: Tell her she can go to hell.

SCOOBY draws a pistol and shoots MAKSIM. He falls. It's too sudden and quick for TANYA to take it in immediately.

SCOOBY: Yeah, I'll tell her, all right. *(To TANYA.)* What's her name?

TANYA lets out a primal scream.

Instant fade.

PART TWO: ESSAYS

GETTING TO KNOW JAMES MACDONALD

Peter Thomson

It is a fact, recorded in one of my notebooks, that I first read a play by James MacDonald in February 1977. It was called *Assumptions About Evelyn Ackroyd*, and written for radio. It had signs, my notebook tells me, of being 'the work of an efficient and experienced writer'. Evelyn Ackroyd is a thirty-three-year-old spinster, but what else is she? That depends on whom you trust. If there is such a thing as an essential self, the young MacDonald seems to be asking, how does it square with other people's views of that self? Who has the better claim to be 'right', Evelyn Ackroyd or the world that summarises her? The discomforting possibility that personal identity is nothing other than a compound of personal appearance and personal circumstance is rarely absent from any of the thirty or so MacDonald plays I've read or seen since 1977: the 'self' as contingent. In November 1977 I read *Zapped*, a highly charged play in which reasons for caring for the disabled are brought into question. The ultra-realistic presentation of the dialogue – clipped and approximate, as in life, and with constant overlapping of speeches – was a feature. MacDonald's achievement was to create complex characters – two young women, both with lesbian yearnings perhaps, and a disabled man. This play would resurface, much changed, in 1985 as *Balance Is Stillness*, and then be again rewritten for publication in *Peering Behind the Curtain* (2002), a volume on the 'extraordinary body', edited by Thomas Fahy and Kimball King. Together with *Crippled Ruth* (1993, published 1996), it represents MacDonald's published 'disability' plays. (*Bread and Circus Freaks*, which appears here, belongs more properly to his 'Russian' plays.)

It's clear from my notebooks that I was wondering what made the author of these two very different plays (*Assumptions* and *Zapped*) tick, and *His Daughters Bury Her*, which I read in December 1978, kept me guessing. There was a *tour de force* of a row between the three daughters in Act Two, and the same scrupulous concern with characterisation. I was evidently reminded, at the time, of Arthur Miller's *The Price*. It is certainly a 'family' drama, and one which shares Miller's preoccupation with the Ibsenite past. If I was wondering what made MacDonald tick, he was evidently wondering the same about his characters. That was about as much as I could say about him. We hadn't, after all, met (so why was I reading his plays?), but we soon would; and the circumstance of our meeting is interesting enough to be worth recording.

Since the year 1975, I had been the first 'reader' of plays submitted through Clive Wolfe to the International Student Playscript Competition, and 1978 was a bumper year. Not only were there sixty-eight entries, but also several of high quality. I despatched, as always, the short-listed texts to Clive, for subsequent semi-final readings (perhaps already by Stephen Jeffreys) preliminary to the final judgement of Alan Ayckbourn, and then got on with my life. But the mills of God grind on, and when the miller is as industrious in the cause of student drama as Clive Wolfe the product is unpredictable. He broached me ('broached' is just the right verb to describe Clive's approach in such matters) with the idea that we might mount rehearsed readings of the short-listed plays at the Northcott Theatre in Exeter. And so – at some time in 1979 – we did. There was another phone-call between the broaching and the event. The relevant bit went something like this:

CLIVE: Have you met James MacDonald?

ME: No.

CLIVE: I'll be interested to know what you make of him.

ME: Why?

CLIVE: Well... put it this way. You may be surprised.

And I suppose I was, though I've known him for so long that it's difficult to recall the first time.

His Daughters Bury Her (I've often been unconvinced by James's titles) was one of the plays given a rehearsed reading. I may have forgotten some of the others. Barry Sutcliffe's *Gerontius* was an obliquely quizzical view of Elgar and his 'public'. Sutcliffe went on to edit a volume of plays by George Colman the Younger and Thomas Morton before setting himself up as a publisher. Now contemplating retirement, he 'blogs' in a website called 'Complete Pants'. Paul Unwin's *Pavilion* was a witty one-act piece in which two very English 'chaps' exposed their prejudices while watching their cricket team being thrashed by a black touring side. Unwin went on to be joint-creator of *Casualty* for the BBC, but would probably rather be remembered for his artistic directorship of the Bristol Old Vic and his superb short film, *Syrup* (1994). And then there was the extraordinary Elizabeth Gowans. She had submitted five plays, all of them worth staging (*Casino* was produced at the Soho Poly in 1992). *The Twain*, which was the one we read, was set in a West Australian Ore Processing Plant, and showed just what a gifted writer could do by interleaving sex and Australian ideals of mateship. Gowans is, I believe, a major writer lost. I 'googled' her, and found only that she had scripted a television mini-series called *Heart of the High Country* (1985). I can't remember whether it was before or after that that she wrote to me from the Raffles Hotel in Singapore, saying that she wasn't planning to write any more. And I met James MacDonald.

To an unpredictable extent, we are what we look like. For all the difference it makes, the abstemious James MacDonald, who is refused service in a pub because he looks drunk to the landlord, is drunk. Very probably, the fact that he walks unsteadily was the first thing I noticed. But it wasn't only appearances that Clive Wolfe was alluding to. When you are confronted with a person whose real life is in his or her writing, the encounter can be disconcerting. It didn't take me long to realize that James (the transition from MacDonald to James begins here) is not a congenitally disabled writer. He is a writer who is congenitally disabled, and that's a different thing. Disability may have knowingly coloured some of his writing, but writing uncoloured by personal experience is as rare as it's boring. We are determined by gender and parentage, by appearance and circumstance (I recently found out who Paris Hilton is), and by what we have so far made of ourselves. By the time I met him, James was decisively a playwright. Peggy Ramsay had noticed that, and signed him up as part of her distinguished list. But a playwright needs confirmation through performance, and Ramsay was not selling James's plays to theatre managements. He registered for a PhD and moved from London (where he'd been seriously mugged) to Exeter (where his only mugging was comparatively frivolous). The move involved his abandoning a thesis on Henry James (Henry James!) and starting one on the little-known Northern Irish playwright, George Shiels (1886–1949). It so happens that Shiels spent most of his adult life in a wheelchair (as the result of an accident, not congenital incapacity), but even if James were to tell me that that was why he was drawn to him, I would have my doubts. Shiels is a mordant comic realist, with an uncultivated eye for the grotesque, and the writing of the thesis coincided with a shift in James's own work, away from realism towards the grotesque. (In a recent letter to me, he has referred to Rabelais and Gogol as 'the patron saints of comic deformity', and he has opened himself to their influence.) This was already evident in the next play I read (in January 1980), *This England*, subsequently rewritten as *Too Many Monkeys* and performed at the Northcott Theatre in November 1983. The family is still a central issue here, but the image is distorted: an unloved and unlovely mother with an epileptic daughter and a disabled son (an expert on the planes of World War Two, who needs his nappy changed). There is a particularly disturbing episode in which the daughter's boyfriend mocks the boy while flirting with his mother: Rabelaisian, James would say, viewing disability from the other side.

From around this time, I date a restlessness in James's writing. *A Nuclear Family* (read in January 1981) is a play of dialogue wars that reach no resolution. How is a playwright to keep on writing without the promise of performance? *Too Many Monkeys* became his favourite, but was that because it was at least staged? The decision to book the Bloomsbury Theatre in London for a short run of *Caliper* in the late summer of 1984 was a bid to bring James to public notice. It didn't work, for any of a number of reasons. There was a student cast (a competent one), and an abrasive central performance from John Hilton (next heard of as a milkman in Lancashire). But this was – like many of James's best plays – a comedy without a distinctive 'feel-good factor'. Peggy Ramsay attended, with a thumbs-down face. Her calculation, I think, was that the punters had no fondness for pieces that knew (and showed) that disabled people can be just as nasty as the rest of us. After that – or so it seemed to me – she abandoned any attempt to sell MacDonald to the professional theatre. Not that he was likely to stop writing (as I've said, that's what he is – a writer). *Self-Service* (read in June 1986) is a complex 'comedy' about graft and corruption among architects and the government in a not-far-distant Britain. *Heavy Petting* (read in February 1987) is a radio play which, like *Caliper*, recognizes, and to some extent relishes, the selfish sexuality of the disabled while at the same time exposing the harmful naivety of the able-bodied (fancy someone in a wheelchair wanting sex!). *Opportunity Knocks* (read in May 1989) is a beautifully crafted one-act piece which focuses on a rent-boy trading in a motorway café. All of these are insistently plays for performance – unperformed. Little wonder that James had accepted a commission to write a small-scale community play for the district of Wonford (Exeter) in 1988. *Women and Children First* deals with Exeter during World War Two, including the impact of Hitler's 1942 Baedeker blitz of the city. Bread and butter work for a frustrated playwright.

Through the 1980s and on into the 1990s, long conversations with James were a constant stimulus to my interest in plays and playwrights. Like all real writers, he lives in the past of his art as well as in the present. It was in December 1990 that I read *The History of Our Dreams*, on the face of it a huge departure from his previous work. The subject here is Stalin, and the treatment owes something to Brechtian epic – one scene after another rather than one scene because of another. In retrospect, I can see the significance of Brecht's probing question – 'who notices what he takes for granted?' – in all the early plays which I have referred to so far. Physical disability had been the vantage-point from which James's mental agility allowed him insights into the unnoticed, but he was uneasy about being labelled as the dramatic spokesman for a misunderstood underclass. (I remember his reluctance to have *Crippled Ruth* staged in the inaugural Platform Four season of 1993, and his response to the success of this exquisite one-act piece included an element of squirming.) The Stalin play, I now believe, marks a point of disjunction in James MacDonald's oeuvre. Increasingly since then, he has sited his sense of otherness (he would, I think, prefer difference) in Russia – particularly in the largely unnoticed (by the western democracies) post-Cold-War Russia. This volume contains three of James's most recent 'Russian' plays. Two earlier ones, *Left-Handed Enterprise* and *Kleptocrats*, were published, under the cover title *As Russia Goes*, in 2000. The first of them had received a staged reading (by the Soho Theatre Company) at the Cockpit in London in 1995. In sum (and the sum is incomplete) these Russian plays constitute a quite extraordinary body of work. I know of nothing like it. Hardy's Wessex? Trollope's Barsetshire? But these are novels – and written from inside their country of origin. James's Russian project is fired, in part, by a wish to impart urgent (before it is too late) information. He has relocated his imagination.

It is possible that the process of relocation began in 1985–6. I had the job of selecting a play for performance by a group of students, six women and six men. There had to be serious acting jobs for all of them, and it was no easy thing to find a text that provided them. Scouting around, I looked at Gorky's last play, *Vassa Zheleznova*. 'Some meaty parts for women – very little for men', I noted in November 1985: 'Could James write a scene for e.g. Polya and Krotkikh: Melnikov and his son: Krotkikh and the Captain: Polya and Yevgeny/Melnikov: the Captain and Ludmila? Or a whole new Act plus an extension of the Captain?' Over the Christmas vacation he did something like that, not according to my prescriptions but growing from them, and we presented Gorky (with MacDonald) in the spring of 1986. It was a much stronger play than Gorky's, and the cast was well above student average (Naomi Cooke, who played Vassa, and Kate Hale, who played her alarmingly powerful secretary, went on to found Foursight Theatre). But the point of significance here is that James had found clues in the text that were invisible to me (and, I suspect, to Gorky, whom he flattered with Gogolian eccentricities). My suspicion is that, between *Vassa Zheleznova* and *The History of Our Dreams*, James's reading took on a decidedly Russian tinge. I remember – but I don't remember when – a conversation about Sukhovo-Kobylin's bizarre trilogy, and I think we both read Erdman's *The Suicide* at much the same time. Certainly he was pressing me into reading Soviet texts which did more for him than they did for me. It was several years later that he made a punishing trip to St. Petersburg, and a little after that that he married a Russian asylum seeker (Inna is now both a source and an addressee of his plays: she has become, in a sense, his muse). His dramatic project has merged with his life.

Teaching in the Exeter Drama Department remains part of that life, too. *The Sweetheart Zone* and *Emigrés* are intriguing products of that. They link back to projects he and I shared: not only *Vassa Zheleznova* but also a dramatisation of *A Tale of Two Cities* from the perspective of the revolutionaries (rather than that of Dickens's middle- and upper-class victims) and the writing of up-to-the-minute Living Newspapers for a pre-determined number (and gender) of actors. These are plays that would not have been written if they were not about to be performed. It's a very obvious point that this harks back to the origins of drama, as well as echoing the practice of contemporary 'fringe' companies. Aeschylus didn't write the *Oresteia* speculatively – and if Shakespeare and Molière had had to have their plays vetted by a selection committee, most of them would have been lost to history. James's early plays, the ones I have briefly described above, are probably, in this sense, 'lost'. The 'wrighting' (in brief contrast to 'writing') of a text-for-performance is a distinct craft, more humble, perhaps, than the art of the dramatist, but not easier. It requires an intuitive relationship with the actor for whom the role is designed. Would Shakespeare have been able to create Hamlet had there been no Burbage? Fighting my way, at a reading, through the individual densities of *The Sweetheart Zone*, I found myself yearning for the clarity of a performance (which, alas, I did not see). It is a text which vibrates with creatable idiosyncrasies, but I find them hard to create for myself in the loneliness of an armchair. *Emigrés* (which I did not see either) is more readily permeable – Russia relocated in a Britain which doesn't know how to assimilate it. But my first encounter with both of these texts served as a Brechtian reminder to take nothing for granted. Am I still getting to know James MacDonald?

I end with another kind of reminiscence. It's March 2002, and I'm in search of the Finborough Theatre in London. It's a city that keeps springing new bits on you, and the new bits blur in with the old. I think I'm right that the theatre is above a pub that stands at the unlikely pinnacle of a triangle of roads. I know that the spectators were seated on two sides of a sparsely furnished room, and that *Bread and Circus Freaks* shared the booking with Christopher Dunkley's *Mirita*. What I seem to remember is that the audience response was respectful, but not fully engaged. Respect is the kind of homage that polite British people pay to disability, and there was Leah Fells (an ex-student James had worked with) embodying disability. I sit in the audience wondering whether we're being really respectful or really patronising (am I remembering the unanticipated surge of fondness I felt for James's wayward first partner when he told me that she'd declined to have his baby because he'd drop it?), and anyway the play isn't about disability – it's about Russia. And it's funny! Not particularly 'feel-good', but definitely funny. So why don't we laugh? There's an ethos of uncertainty about just what the play is doing. (The same thing happened as long ago as *Caliper*.) Whoever this 'MacDonald' is, he doesn't write according to a discernible emotional formula. I leave feeling vaguely dissatisfied, not with the actors' performance so much as with my own. Only later do I learn that the last-night audience found its way to relax into laughter, thereby releasing the play. Martin Harvey has suggested to me that the laughter was led by his old mentor, the inspirational Hungarian director George Roman, and by George's Hungarian wife. Maybe you have to know something about 'the other side' – feel something from the other side – to appreciate fully any of James's plays. Or maybe you have to act in them.

Director's Notes

Martin Harvey

In the early 'nineties I was working on a production of *Of Mice and Men* for the Belgrade Theatre in Coventry. I had asked James to come and speak to the cast, to give them a literary, political and historical context to the piece. James spoke at the read-through to an enthusiastic and talented group of actors, who were eager to pick his brains further in the pub that evening. The Belgrade had booked James into a hotel in the centre of town; and so, after one of those great evenings in which it is possible to see a company forming in front of your eyes, we put James into a taxi to take him to his hotel.

The next morning James relayed a story which will remain with me to the end of my days: the night manager refused him entrance to the hotel until he had taken him to an ATM to withdraw the cash for the night's accommodation (even though this had been booked and payment agreed by the theatre). If James is on his own, he is often mistaken for a drunk (even though he very rarely takes alcohol), a tramp, an idiot, an untouchable; the night manager probably saw him as all of these. This is how James had to pay for his determination to remain independent. Needless to say, the theatre took the hotel to task and, as a reinforcement of his independence, James insisted on staying there again on a subsequent visit to the cast. This time he was given red carpet treatment, with which he was clearly unimpressed.

I relate this story because I think it gives insight into James's world and more specifically into where his writing is coming from and the characters, situations and settings that interest him. These plays are peopled by outsiders, misfits, those who are often regarded as non-persons; the wrongly labelled who have to fight in order just to validate their existence, and ask for little else but to be regarded as genuinely useful contributors to the communities in which they find themselves and from which they are often, in one way or another, excluded.

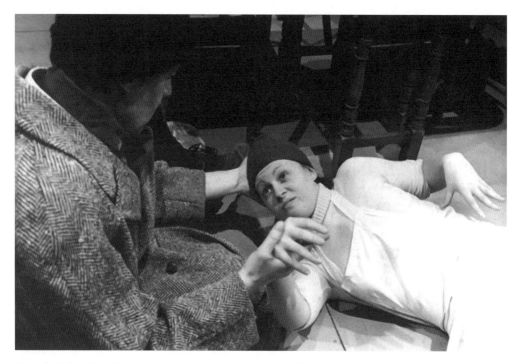

Osip (Michael Bottle) and Inna (Leah Fells) after a fall. *Bread and Circus Freaks*, Finborough Theatre, March 2002. Photo: Marilyn Kingwill

Given the central motif linking the plays which appear in this volume (and others which do not), one might expect these 'outsiders' to be treated with kid gloves, ennobled, even sanitized. Far from it, no holds are barred; these characters inhabit a world which is grotesque, where body-image and bodily functions are foregrounded, heightened and celebrated. At the climax of *Bread and Circus Freaks* Osip Pischik and Inna thrash around on the floor together in a comically grotesque dance, which is not intended to elicit pity but rather freedom through laughter.

In another play of James's, *The Monkey Sanctuary*, this grotesque celebration of the disabled body reaches its peak in a scene where a disabled man, shut away from society, is given a very rough but highly sexually charged bath by the woman of his dreams. She is Russian and she deals with him and his genitals without a trace of coyness or circumspection. It is this frankness which holds the key to the 'Russia' question. I too have asked James on numerous occasions, 'Why another play set in Russia?' (He even wrote a play set in Chicago to shut me up.) Since directing *Bread and Circus Freaks*, I have come to a much clearer understanding of the driving force behind this issue.

James does not labour under some delusion that disabled people and other marginals are treated more fairly, with more kindness, or are given more value in Russia than anywhere else;

in fact, from his own experiences, he may well believe the reverse to be true. What he has been attracted by is a culture, which he views as robust, containing prejudice which is expressed openly and not sanitized by English niceties or American correctness; emotions which are fully expressed and which can swing violently from tears or anger to laughter in a moment; and where the taboos surrounding the body are non-existent. He has found here a world where natural reality can be exaggerated, distorted and ultimately exploded, so as to be re-assembled into a different kind of truth, fuelled by imagination.

This place may not be *Russia* at all, in the sense of a country we can objectively find, but more a place which is created from stories; stories from literature or true stories orally related, distorted and coloured in the telling. In short, it is a place of the imagination, based on observable truths, then taken beyond them into a kind of dreamscape. The physical settings in which these *dreams* take place are outside the mainstream of life, in Russia or elsewhere: a cut-off village; the nebulous world of hostels and shady hotels, inhabited by those without the correct papers; a work camp for women, where the very rules of existence can change in the blink of an eye.

It is not my intention here to indulge in detailed literary criticism of these plays (my contact with them has been far too visceral for that), more to give a context through which to understand their style, which has proved to be increasingly important for me in their production. My principal concerns are with approaches to acting, from preparation, through rehearsal, to performance, and with the relationship between actors and audience.

All characters are real. That is to say, they are based on a perceived reality. Many of them have, at their core, true stories made up from observed incidents, related histories, documentary evidence. The basis for the setting of *Bread and Circus Freaks* comes from a documentary film about the bread train and the irascible woman who sells the bread, which has to be pushed into the village. The actor playing Pania starts from there and from the invented fragments of the character's related history, her time in the pioneers, her marriage, her abortion, her schooldays etc., and weaves these together into a sense of character. This, of course, conforms to the first principles of Stanislavskian work, namely to look for the *given circumstances* and, because the plays are made up from many stories, there is a wealth of potential *given circumstance*. Problems, however, may arise if those circumstances are not treated with some latitude, and the actor should be aware that a slavish attempt to weave them together into a linear structure or *through-line* may lead to frustration. Stories may only be half true, they may be exaggerated, they may be a deliberate fabrication, so looking for cut and dried consistency is dangerous. But half-truth, exaggeration and fabrication only deal with truth as fact; behind each one of them is another truth, the truth of imagination.

It may be that this nether world, somewhere between the real and the imagined, is a place where greater truths can be explored, away from the crippling exactitudes of bare fact and recordable history. In *Bread and Circus Freaks*, Inna breaks out of her physical disability as she describes her journey in search of her mother. Here truth, desire, fear and resolution are manufactured by Inna as she seeks to create her own space, her own voice, independent of those who are fighting for the right to speak for her. When Osip proposes to Inna and calls her his ideal, he is reaching for a world in his imagination, where he is no longer marginalized but can be validated through caring and being cared for. The actor must find the comfort in the desire for sanctuary and not in some physical or sexual imperative. If the others misread him, Inna understands.

In order for the actors to be able to play all this, it is necessary to search for a coherent style beyond naturalism. These are not characters, separated from the audience, going about their lives with consistency, unaware of their theatrical and imaginative context. There is a playfulness and improvisational quality which requires a conscious contact. Neither is the work confrontational, requiring that kind of head-on contact which pushes an audience back on its heels, shaming them into complicity or creating brutal alienation. This is more by way of an invitation, a suggested complicity. I imagine the audience as another character, as if on stage, with whom all is shared, sometimes directly – never as an aside, everybody in the space, audience included, shares in everything. (In *The Sweetheart Zone*, James takes this a step further and gives the audience a defined character, that of a body of observers, constantly present and visible to the characters on stage.)

This requires a strong sense of shared space and even, to some extent, shared light. When we produced *Bread and Circus Freaks* at the Finborough, we worked in traverse, audience facing each other across the playing space. Rather than the usual black-box studio, we painted the whole space blue and, although concentrating light on the playing space, allowed a diffuse light to illuminate the audience and the wall behind. The intention was to give a sense of one space, without division, into which we had all been invited.

The consequent required style of playing can be tricky for the actors to find, particularly for those used to hiding behind character or metaphorical footlights. An easy acceptance of the presence of the audience and an easy communication with them, once found, allows actors and audience alike to enter, enjoy, and reflect upon the imaginative world of the play. When hit upon well, this style works as a release mechanism on actor and audience alike, and we found that, as we got more and more at home with it during the run of performances and more and more relaxed in the relationship with the audience, the more the grotesque nature of the piece could be released, without jarring, and the funnier it became.

If this style can be tricky for accomplished professionals to find (and I don't think we could have wished for a better cast than played *Bread and Circus Freaks* at the Finborough) it is quite a demand to make of students. Nevertheless we were keen to pursue the idea in *Émigrés* and *The Sweetheart Zone,* both of which formed the culminating project for the *Interpretative Acting* module which James and I have been teaching together for the past few years at Exeter University. Both plays were, in fact, written specifically for the students on the module and aimed (amongst other things) to bring together workshops undertaken throughout the module.

The module, which aims to teach approaches to acting with text, begins with naturalism and with *An Actor Prepares* by Konstantin Stanislavski. The students grapple with *given circumstances, the magic if, emotion memory* etc., endeavouring to work the theory into acting naturalistic texts ranging from Chekhov to Wesker. It is not an intensive acting course (nor could it ever be, lasting as it does, over one university semester), but rather seeks to introduce the students to a range of ideas, which are worked on practically, and from which they can begin to assemble a *toolbox* with which to approach their work on text. After work on Stanislavski, there are workshops on Michael Chekhov's techniques, Shakespeare and verse handling, and Bertolt Brecht (on which subject they mainly come to university armed with misunderstandings given to them at school).

The work on a play by James follows on from this, giving the students a chance to gain a sense of company, ensemble and indeed ownership of the work. In feedback, which we ask for at the end of the module, this project always rates highly with them, both for the challenges it lays down and for the excitement it generates. Each year, it seems, the project has become more ambitious, starting out three years ago with *Émigrés,* which was presented, in edited form, as a script-in-hand rehearsed reading, to *The Sweetheart Zone* which, in early 2007, was presented as an off-text studio production.

The plays present a number of challenges for the students beyond acting style. Firstly, the subject matter: the students have already, within workshops on Brecht, been asked to consider the political content of a piece (usually a short scene from, say, *The Caucasian Chalk Circle*) and to come to a collective view of what that content is and how to present it; now they are asked to consider the entire content of a new play in what is now a large group or company. For *Émigrés* we had a sometimes heated debate on the subjects of immigration and asylum-seekers; for *The Sweetheart Zone,* the debate ranged from the nature of power and its abuses, to the problems of the outsider and bullying.

Secondly, the very act of working with a new text brings with it disciplines for the students to master (disciplines which many professionals have problems with), namely coping with a changing text, understanding the actor's role in shaping that text, and simply playing a role that has no history of being played before. This last carries with it a responsibility to the play and the text which they may not have encountered before. Often these days, and very often within the university context, texts are viewed as merely starting points from which to create something new; but in the first outing of a new text, the job is to expose the play. Read any review of a modern production of a Shakespeare play and it will talk about the production, the performances, and the interpretation. A review of a new work deals first and foremost with that work, as there is no history of productions against which to measure interpretation.

Thirdly, because of the size of the groups that take this module, and because of James's refusal to be beaten by cast size and gender split, the students are asked to work in a large ensemble, a task which taxes the powers of concentration, generosity and listening. The fact that the students have managed this task so well is not only a tribute to their own ability to find generous ways of working, but also to James's generosity of spirit, in the writing, in rehearsal, in the re-writing and as an audience of his own work, which has now become the work of many.

James moreover uses the creation of this text to bring together the different strands followed throughout the course. So the actors have to develop a sense of their character's history; many of them have stories to tell, which may, as in *Bread and Circus Freaks* be embellished fact (but are mainly based on real-life stories that have been related to James). They have to understand how their character and their stories fit the project of the play and what we, as a company, have collectively agreed we are trying to say with it. They have to communicate that in an easy but direct relationship with an audience which must be included. Above all, in such a large ensemble, each must take responsibility to keep the focus clear and moving towards the climactic moment. This moment, when Zhenia, in *The Sweetheart Zone*, is forced to cross the stage, unaided and with all eyes on her, brings together in a single *gestus* the cruelty of the bully to the outsider. One might even say that, distilled in this moment, are all the moments in James's life which resemble the moment in Coventry when he was marched to the ATM.

Professionals and students alike who have encountered these plays have found them very rewarding to work on. They have depth, humour, complexity of style and the kind of language that actors like, namely the kind of language they love to speak but for the most part could not write themselves. As a director, I can say that they have all presented me with something to learn and something to say. I commend them to you.

Freaks, Food and Fairy Tales: Confronting the Limits of Disability in Bread and Circus Freaks

Thomas Fahy

Tapping into the tradition of the carnival and vaudeville, James MacDonald's *Bread and Circus Freaks* offers a powerful critique of the social prejudices that limit, restrict, and interpret the disabled body. The entire work is set in Pania Andreyevna's bread shop. Pania claims that she was a close friend of Inna's mother, and for this reason, she has agreed to give Inna, a twenty-year-old girl with cerebral palsy, a job there. With Inna's disability as the centrepiece, the play depicts four people who enter the shop in succession and ultimately define themselves in relation to Inna and her body – Pania (her aggressive employer whose verbal cruelty seems to be fuelled by the psychological burden of her abortion), Marianna Seligman (a former art teacher who tries to compensate for her failures as a mother by pressuring Inna to go to art school), Osip Pishchik (a vagrant whose romantic obsession with Inna began when she was institutionalized as a young girl), and Volkov (an ex-military constable who represents the government's oppressive authority). MacDonald uses each character to depict the ways in which many people – even when they believe themselves to be well intentioned – tend to equate disability with helplessness, dependence, and even personal failure.

His critique of this equation announces itself most clearly through the play's ironic humour, much of which comes from the fact that the true 'freaks' on stage are the able-bodied characters, whose attitudes about society and difference feed into self-destructive delusions. In fact, the word 'freak' only appears once in the play itself, and it is applied to the people who run government institutions for the disabled: 'Did those freaks let him handle you? [...] Those guardians you say were like sadists' (47). Freakishness, MacDonald suggests through this pointed use of the word, is about treating difference inhumanely, not about the body itself.

Mikhail Bakhtin's oft-discussed notion of the carnivalesque can provide an effective starting point for understanding MacDonald's use of freakishness here. As Bakhtin explains, the carnival provides an accepted outlet for the lower classes to satirize the wealthy and privileged. It inverts power structures that reinforce social hierarchies – allowing participants to parody the excesses of political power, affluence, and physical difference. In fact, Bakhtin's *Rabelais and His World* reminds us that the carnivalesque contains an important 'bodily element' (19). The masks and disguises of the carnival typically play into anxieties about the body – degradation, irregularity, carnality, defecation and mortality. But these images are only meant to be temporary. Costumes can be taken off and put away. According to Bakhtin, 'carnival is not spectacle seen by the people; they live it, and everyone participates because its very idea embraces all the people. While carnival lasts, there is no other life outside it' (7). Outside the performance and laughter of the carnival, therefore, the body is expected to be contained and controlled. But the visibly disabled body does not allow this containment; it operates as an unwanted reminder of bodily degradation and irregularity. And this is one of the concerns taken up in MacDonald's play, whose protagonist, Inna, has been institutionalized for much of her childhood because of her disability.

MacDonald also explores this concern through his use of traditions associated with vaudeville – a popular form of entertainment in the nineteenth and early twentieth centuries that was comprised of various performance styles, such as burlesque, freak shows, minstrelsy and musical numbers. As part of the theatrical productions of the American Museum, for example, P. T. Barnum crafted *entr'acte* vaudeville that featured singers, blackface, jugglers, and some of his more famous freak performers, including Henry Johnson ('What Is It?') and Tom Thumb, who was billed as the smallest man in the world. The incorporation of freak shows into vaudeville further reinforced the ways in which the extraordinary body was viewed as a form of entertainment. Scholars such as Leslie Fiedler, Robert Bogdan, Rosemarie Garland Thomson, Rachel Adams and others have shown that the freak represented the Other for the audience. The performer's body became a visible marker for exclusion, and it often reinforced the audience's own sense of belonging to a group different from the one onstage – a more 'perfect' group. At the same time, Thomson argues that the audience both despised and identified with the Other: 'the spectator enthusiastically invested his dime in the freak show not only to confirm his own superiority, but also to safely focus an identificatory longing upon these creatures who embodies freedom's elusive and threatening promise of not being like everybody else' (*Extraordinary Bodies* 69). In other words, the viewer's longing for freedom from the quotidian as well as from social norms was an integral part of this exchange.

Certainly, the title of MacDonald's play invites these historical comparisons. It not only alludes to the Latin phrase *panem et circenses* (bread and circuses) from Juvenal's *Satire X* – which criticizes both the government's use of entertainment and food to distract the public from more pressing socio-political concerns and the public's complacent acceptance of this – but the addition of the word 'freaks' also announces the focus of MacDonald's social critique. His work addresses the problems of equating disability with spectacle. More specifically, through a vaudevillian sequence of unrelated interactions and a thematic link between food and community, *Bread and Circus Freaks* provides a dramatic mosaic that challenges the audience to confront extreme versions of their own biases and to reject the historical association between disability and freakishness.

Not enough brown: the hunger for acceptance and belonging

Throughout the play, MacDonald uses food as a central metaphor for the often unacknowledged needs and desires of the disabled. All of the characters hunger for something – a job, a cause, independence, love, justice – to give their lives meaning. Yet in a work whose title and setting suggest the importance of literal food, it is notable that no one eats. The bread shop merely distributes food. Nothing is baked or made there. And if we are to believe Pania's complaints about the shortage of brown bread and the mouldy condition of the white, this bread shop also fails to provide sustenance for the community.

Bread doesn't offer nourishment here, and it also doesn't forge the kind of social bonds that are traditionally associated with the sharing of food. As E. N. Anderson explains in *Everybody Eats: Understanding Food and Culture*, 'food is used in every society to communicate messages. Pre-eminent among these are messages of group solidarity; food sharing is literally sacred in almost all religions and takes on a near-sacred quality in many (most?) families around the world' (7). He goes on to argue that:

> one main message of food [...] is solidarity. Eating together means sharing and participating. [...] The other main message is separation. Food marks social class, ethnicity, and so on. Food transactions define families, networks, friendship groups, religions, and virtually every other socially institutionalized group. Naturally, one group can try to use food to separate itself, while another is trying to use food to eliminate that separation. (125)

This tension between solidarity and separation is certainly evident in MacDonald's play – where the characters desire community but largely seem isolated from one another. And the lack of food sharing and consumption reinforces this.

MacDonald specifically links literal/metaphoric hunger with loneliness in order to highlight the importance of a more inclusive community – one that acknowledges and treats disability with open-mindedness and compassion. At the outset of the play, Pania reminds Inna that having a job prevents her from being 'an outcast, for people to take pity on or worse ... because pity soon turns to contempt ... and then you might starve' (13). Being an outcast leads to social and literal starvation here. Yet Pania, who later reveals that she had an abortion after her husband left her, is arguably a marginalized figure as well. The lack of intimacy in her life is highlighted humorously by her reaction to the goats having sex outside the bread shop: 'There's no men, just like there's not enough brown. So what's the point of liking sex?' (18). Food and sex are in short supply in Pania's world, and this prevents her from finding pleasure in life. It also keeps her emotionally distant from the community she lives in and serves. Not surprisingly, she has internalized an adversarial relationship with her customers – relying on a rifle ('hunter') to quell potentially violent crowds. These qualities make her far less connected to the community than Inna, who has several visitors throughout the play. Nevertheless, Pania throws out the words 'cripple', 'outcast' and 'pariah' like punches to remind Inna of her othered status – a status that is inescapable because of her body.

This solidarity/separation dichotomy gets reinforced through the image of bread as well, which tends to foster a violent competitiveness among people, not solidarity ('They'll be asking for bread … and then taking our blood just as soon as we've run out' [14]). Pania, for example, is a seller of bread, a provider, and she views this profession as having an important social value. She repeatedly tells stories of her own physical strength (pushing the bread train and lifting the heavy trays) to remind Inna of her limitations as an individual and her failure to contribute something meaningful to society. It is not surprising, therefore, that Pania refuses to let Inna do any physical work. She needs Inna to remain a foil for her own sense of productivity and usefulness. At one point, she even offers Inna some brown bread in a gesture that amounts to a handout – negating Inna's desire to work.

INNA: No, I don't want – [...] No, of course I eat bread, but I have no objection to the white loaf.

PANIA: Unlike the rest of us. Aren't you human? Look here … *(Showing her.)* It's mouldy. There's gobs of mould here and here. [...]

INNA *(Taking the white loaf.)*: It's not that bad. Look, I can cut the bits off. *(Inspects.)* I think you must be exaggerating. I don't see any –

PANIA: I think you must be dim-witted or something, not to want brown and then not to see any fault in the white. (23)

For Pania, difference exists only in extremes (brown/white, right/wrong, human/disabled). It requires the absolute rejection of one thing over the other – so that one cannot refuse to eat brown bread without seeing the white as flawed. Likewise, one cannot accept difference (in terms of disability, sexuality, ethnicity, etc.) without calling into question accepted notions of normality. Hence, Inna must stay an isolated figure. To preserve Pania's sense of social importance/relevance, Inna must be seen as a 'cripple' and by implication subhuman.

MacDonald continues to explore this tension between separation and solidarity through two figures (the artist and the lover) that reject food in order to follow their passions. Of course, *Bread and Circus Freaks* is not *commedia dell'arte*, and MacDonald offers inventive variations on these types to highlight age-old prejudices that still limit the disabled. First of all, Marianna, Inna's former art teacher, tries to direct young people to pursue the arts. Here, she purchases bread as a pretence for speaking with Inna – in an attempt to nurture/nourish her. Marianna has secured a scholarship for Inna, and, presenting Frida Kahlo as a model, she urges Inna to develop her art. 'Go to art school, test yourself, if you want to find out what you're really worth'

(34). On the surface, Marianna seems to have Inna's best interests in mind, but her own attitudes about disability are not so different from Pania's. She fundamentally believes that Inna's 'worth' is in question, yet she hopes that art will remedy this to some extent. Art can give Inna a place in society by providing an outlet to transform her disability into something aesthetic, as Kahlo did. In other words, art can provide a way for Inna to define herself completely by her disability. At one point, Marianna snaps at Pania: 'And just how do you think she can help you? You need a strong, healthy girl for work of that kind. Could she push the bread train? You know she couldn't' (36). Inna replies that she 'wanted to' and that she yearns for an 'ordinary job', but Marianna can't hear this. For her, Inna doesn't need a practical existence, as represented by jobs and bread; she needs the protection of educators and social workers. She needs an outlet – art – to define herself entirely by her own body.

Marianna's failure stems, in part, from the fact that she already sees Inna as an art object, and MacDonald presents this desire to read/interpret disability (as opposed to seeing the individual) as one of the impediments that prevent the disabled from achieving a broader social acceptance. Marianna's initial interest in Inna, for example, comes from the way her body reminds Marianna of Diego Velázquez's *Las Meninas*: 'And that painting by Velázquez – the group portrait with the little girl who's adored by the dwarf. [...] The aristocracy always looked after their lame ones ... like beloved family pets. It wasn't looked on as misfortune to be lame. [...] I want to look after you, darling' (40). For Marianna, Inna's body represents need and dependency. It relegates her to the realm of the metaphoric. On one hand, Marianna wants to recast the Velázquez with Inna as family pet and herself as the beneficent aristocrat. On the other hand, Marianna reads Inna's body as an image for the failures of Russia more broadly. 'It's the condition of Russia, my dear. People become friends with their condition ... They depend on it, finally become enslaved by it. Like the people in this village. [...] You do nothing, quite frankly, to help yourselves' (42). Both of these interpretations suggest that disability is either a condition that requires the magnanimous assistance of the able-bodied or something that must be overcome. It never occurs to Marianna to accept Inna (or her own daughter) for who she is – an individual with her own desires and goals. Instead, she warns Inna that to accept her disability is to be trapped by it.

MacDonald presents the lover figure, Osip, as another example of how disability is often read in aesthetic and metaphoric terms. Even though Osip is a vagrant, he isn't interested in eating bread. Instead, he hungers for intimacy and connection, just as he longs to relive the time when he performed magic tricks for institutionalized children. That was a period in his life when he felt as if he were making a meaningful contribution to others. His love for Inna is not only an attempt to compensate for this loneliness (as well as his social status as a pariah), but it also comes from his idealization of her. He calls her 'a living portrait, [...] a tiny masterpiece' (48), and 'an angel' (58). The latter invokes another clichéd view of disability: reading the extraordinary body in terms of the divine. Ancient Greek and Roman society, for example, interpreted natural phenomena as the result of cosmic or divine forces: fires, epidemics, the appearance of a comet or eclipse and the birth of an extraordinary body were believed to presage the doom of an empire and the breakdown of social order. Similarly in the Middle Ages, Christians viewed disabled bodies as divine warnings against the dangers of pride, disobedience and waning faith. Osip parrots these interpretations explicitly: 'She needs to be recognized for what she is. [...] That's right ... she is – a message from God for the nation' (59). The problem here (other than the fact that he is thirty years her senior and that they first met when she was a child) is that Osip views her disability as a kind of panacea for his own suffering. Like Pania and Marianna, he insists that Inna's body proves a level of suffering worse than his own. Her body, therefore, evinces her need for help: 'I love you, my little Inyechka. You're my ideal, you are! [...] Let me help you. You've suffered more than the rest of us' (57). Throughout *Bread and Circus Freaks*, it is this kind of selfish need to feel better off than someone else that drives the characters' obsession with disability.

All of the able-bodied characters fail to see Inna's basic hunger – her desire to be needed. At one point, she tells Pania: 'Now I can see that you need me. Oh, how you've suffered in life. I can see what they mean now – Pania Andreyevna, the Bread Lady. What a glorious thing to be needed for life!' (57). Pania (a name which may be an allusion to the Pania in Maori mythology who was betrayed by her husband when he placed food in her mouth to prevent her from returning to the sea) is the 'bread lady'. Her place in this village is clearly established, and Inna desires exactly this – a meaningful, recognized role in society that has nothing to do with her body. At the end of the play, she does find an outlet for this – Osip. When Volkov, the constable, threatens to arrest him, Inna offers to be his caretaker. 'He's a menace', Volkov explains. 'They all are, people like him [...] I mean, look at him, dear. He's disgusting' (63). Inna immediately recognizes that the language Volkov applies to Osip has also been used to describe her: 'I was judged a pariah ... unclean. They locked me up for years, too' (63). Inna has successfully fought this kind of prejudice throughout her life. She has, in effect, forged a community of her own. She has found a job, turned away the assistance of Marianna, and become the caretaker–lover of Osip. None of these things has changed society's view of her, however. Pania still sees her as a cripple, and her decision to help Osip does seem to run counter to her earlier desire 'to move on my own first ... learn who I am in the world. I've been sheltered all my life, really sheltered' (59). Perhaps, this is MacDonald's point. She may not be sheltered any longer, but she will always be subject to the Panias, Mariannas, and Volkovs of the world. Nevertheless, these prejudices don't have to limit Inna, MacDonald suggests. Her choice to be with Osip offers a hopeful alternative. In spite of the limitations placed on her, she still has the ability to be compassionate, to help ease the suffering of those around her.

MacDonald's introduction of Volkov broadens the critique of his play, moving it from the problems with individual prejudices against disability (seeing the extraordinary body in terms of spectacle) to an indictment of the systemic practices that attempt to render disability invisible. As an ex-military figure and village constable, Volkov represents the law in its strictest, most unyielding form. Like the banking uniform that Gregor Samsa's father wears in Kafka's *Metamorphosis*, Volkov's uniform – along with his hateful words and abusive actions – makes him a symbol for legally sanctioned oppression and violence. His desire to remove 'people like' Osip (the homeless, the sick, the disabled) 'for [their] own protection' (63) is not only arrogant and spiteful, but it is also callous. He judges Osip on appearance alone, just as Pania judges Inna's job at the bakery as an act in the circus (40). MacDonald clearly crafts *Bread and Circus Freaks* to attack this kind of politics of visibility. It was through a similar legerdemain of costuming, rehearsed behaviour, spiel and true-life pamphlets that freak show entrepreneurs like Barnum created 'freaks' – dressing up African Americans as Fiji cannibals and using padded clothing to make a performer the fattest woman in the world, for example. This link between Inna and a circus act, therefore, illustrates the terrible legacy of the freak show and how it continues to shape social attitudes about disability.

Volkov's (and by extension the government's) main response to difference, however, is to render it invisible. As a society, we put criminals behind bars not only as a means of punishment but also as an act of erasure – removing them from sight. In *Crime and Punishment in America*, for example, Elliot Currie discusses the effects of this in the United States:

> Our growing reliance on incarceration helps us avoid confronting a host of deep and stubborn social problems. [...] A swollen correctional system allows us to sweep these problems under the rug, but it does not make them go away, and indeed makes them worse. (191)

MacDonald's play offers a similar warning about the institutionalization of the disabled in the post-Soviet era. It only heightens the challenges facing this community because it provides an official stamp for labelling anyone who is different as an enemy of the state and of the social order.

Disability and rewriting fairy tales

You don't have to read more than a few pages of Grimm's fairy tales to find acts of violence, cruelty, and vengeance associated with food. The queen in 'Snow White' – who uses an apple to poison Snow White – is eventually tortured to death with red-hot, iron shoes. Hansel and Gretel, whose parents have abandoned them in the woods because they are too poor to provide them with bread – ultimately kill the witch who plans to eat them. And the stepsisters in 'Cinderella' throw peas and lentils into the ashes for Cinderella to pick up. At the end of the story, they mutilate their feet to trick the prince into marrying them and are blinded for their wickedness. MacDonald taps into this tradition throughout *Bread and Circus Freaks*. Food often represents a longing for happiness in fairy tales, but the dangers of hunger are never far off. MacDonald uses the threat of danger/violence in this play to rewrite the fairy tale in terms of disability. Inna, a poor girl who works in a bread shop, is the princess/maiden of this play. Her parents are absent, and she hungers for something more in life. But it is not external beauty that defines her; it is her disability. MacDonald asks us to consider the implications of this inversion. Snow White, for example, is spared her life and helped time and time again because of her stunning beauty. Inna, on the other hand, is continually restricted by her physical appearance. She remains a perpetual outcast and circus act. She is not locked in a tower but an institution – a period in her life that she ironically calls 'a fairy tale' (48). Nor does a prince rescue her. Instead she must rescue the homeless, emasculated Osip.

The version of romance that MacDonald presents here reinforces the idea that traditional fairytale narratives are not available to the disabled. Inna may dream of princes on horseback, but Pania repeatedly transforms fantasies of romanticized love into stories of rape.

PANIA: You like soldiers, do you? You'd like to be raped by a soldier? [...] Is that your schoolgirl fantasy, is it? Foreign war with Russian soldiers raping the flesh off you? Sex isn't that good.

INNA: That's not my fantasy, Madame Pania.

PANIA: Ha – says you.

INNA: It must be yours.

PANIA: It's nobody's, that's the whole point. (16)

Pania's fantasy rejects the romance of fairy tales for all women, but she suggests that the impediments to love are greater for the disabled – always alluding to the dangerous wolves that lurk outside the bread shop. Little Red Riding Hood may have been tricked by a wolf to stray from the path to grandmother's house, but this beautiful girl is still able to escape his treachery with the help of a huntsman. From Pania's perspective, Inna cannot stray from the path of her condition and expect to be saved. The wolves (outside world) will quickly tear her to pieces if she no longer has a job (the protection of the able-bodied). MacDonald's rewriting of such fairytale narratives and images suggests how far the disabled experience is removed from mainstream culture and society.

In a 2002 interview, James MacDonald lamented the failures of British society to deal with difference and the need more broadly for disability to be recognized and dealt with humanely. 'If people can't even acknowledge it, how can they engage with it to overcome the problem? We are still dealing with the difference thrown up by class barriers, so others – sexual, ethnic, and physical – must be some way off being addressed. Things have improved. Disabled people are now generally visible at least. But being accepted remains a future stage of progress; how far in the future I don't know' (Fahy and King, *Peering Behind the Curtain*, 112). His call for acceptance drives *Bread and Circus Freaks*. This powerful play challenges audiences to see the ways in which prejudices and misguided altruism limit the disabled. His use of humour also reminds us that it's okay to laugh. Ultimately, laughter might be the best tool for helping us recognize the absurdity of our own biases and to do something about it.

Works Consulted

Adams, Rachel (2001), *Sideshow U.S.A.: Freaks and the American Cultural Imagination*, Chicago: University of Chicago Press.

Allen, Robert C. (1991), *Horrible Prettiness: Burlesque and American Culture*, Chapel Hill: University of North Carolina Press.

Anderson, E. N. (2005), *Everybody Eats: Understanding Food and Culture*, New York: New York University Press.

Bakhtin, Mikhail (1984), *Rabelais and His World*, (trans. Hélène Iswolsky), Bloomington: Indiana University Press.

Bogdan, Robert (1988), *Freak Show: Presenting Human Oddities for Amusement and Profit*, Chicago: University of Chicago Press.

Currie, Elliot (1998), *Crime and Punishment in America*, New York: Metropolitan Books.

Fahy, Thomas (2006), *Freak Shows and the Modern American Imagination: Constructing the Damaged Body from Willa Cather to Truman Capote*, New York: Palgrave Macmillan.

Fahy, Thomas and Kimball King (eds.) (2002), *Peering Behind the Curtain: Disability, Illness, and the Extraordinary Body in Contemporary Theater*, New York: Routledge.

Fiedler, Leslie (1978), *Freaks: Myths and Images of the Secret Self*, New York: Simon and Schuster.

Harris, Neil (1973), *Humbug: The Art of P. T. Barnum*, Boston: Little, Brown.

Lott, Eric (1993), *Love and Theft: Blackface Minstrelsy and the American Working Class*, New York: Oxford University Press.

Reiss, Benjamin (2001), *The Showman and the Slave: Race, Death, and Memory in Barnum's America*, Cambridge, MA: Harvard University Press.

Thomson, Rosemarie Garland (1997), *Extraordinary Bodies: Figuring Physical Disability in American Culture and Literature*, New York: Columbia University Press.

—— (1996), 'Introduction: From Wonder to Error – A Genealogy of Freak Discourse in Modernity', in Rosemarie Garland Thomson (ed.), *Freakery: Cultural Spectacles of the Extraordinary Body*, New York: New York University Press, 1–19.

Wilson, Dudley (1993), *Signs and Portents: Monstrous Births from the Middle Ages to the Enlightenment*, New York: Routledge.

EPILOGUE

Su Elliott

I read *Bread and Circus Freaks* again the other day to refresh my memory of Pania Andreyevna and the play. I'd forgotten (how could I?) how very, very funny it is and what a complex and interesting character *she* is.

I don't know how I 'approach' a part. I like to read the play myself and then enjoy the actual first-day play-reading with the rest of the cast, and then sort of get stuck in. But there are two really vital elements that make your life oh-so-much easier, and these are a good director who isn't going to flaunt his/her ego and who has plenty of ideas *and* a good script. Well, we actors were lucky in *Bread and Circus Freaks* as we had both in spades.

People aren't Mr Men. You can't say someone is just nasty. They may be, in certain circumstances, and your subjective view of them may not change from that. But in your heart you know that there are people who find the person fun or helpful or warm. It's the same in theatre; but with James the complexities of the characters are already written in, and that's so much fun to work on. Though as with any good piece of writing, there's plenty to discover along the way that isn't immediately obvious, and of course the audience will find their own insights.

I loved the monumental selfishness of Pania. If she thinks she's not getting enough attention, she practically says, 'Well, that's enough about me, now what about *ME*?' She can be cruel. She *wants* to be cruel, and she's very hard on Inna, but then again, it's a hard life and a hard place to live, and she knows that. It's 'tough love', as we would call it now, but as you work into the play, you can see that there is kindness there, and there are absolutely no pretensions whatsoever. The exchanges with Marianna were particularly fun to do. Pania certainly knows more than she lets on – after all, she makes reference to Kandinsky. But of course it doesn't suit her to be on the same intellectual footing with Marianna: she'd lose the argument then, and she needs to have the upper hand at all times. When Pania's logic is sliding all over the place as she duets and dives in this rapid-fire argument, Marianna says, 'You just detest giving in' – an understatement if ever there was one. I loved the lack of relaxation in Pania, the competitiveness, and how anyone encountering her has to be on their toes. Nothing came easy to this woman, so why should it come easy to anyone else? She's like a recalcitrant teenager. You can hear her saying, 'Yeah, yeah, whatever', and having an answer for everything.

When she's with Pishchik, she matches his slyness; but it's then in the script that James gives the information that her husband has left her and that there is a deep hurt there. But James isn't finished, because *then* you realize that she's had an abortion, which reverts to her line early on, 'Oh, yes, my insides still work', and is one of the keys to the way she reacts, and to her own pain.

I can't remember any difficulties working on and performing this piece, apart from the fact that we could have done with a bit more time. The style of acting suited me very well. I'm rather partial to confronting an audience head-on – as Pania does. It calls for a mixture of confrontation and charm; otherwise they'll be put off. The humour (here) helps, and it's such fun to do. I loved the line about Pioneers being Organized Criminals, like everybody...(*Ghoulish pause*.)...only smaller. There are loads like that – too many to quote here. I do know that when you work on a play, you're all in it together – the crew, the cast, the writer and the director, and when it works (together with the audience), it becomes more than the sum of its parts, and that's when it takes off and you know it was a Good Job Done. But it's a hell of a lot easier when you've got a good script to start with. So...thanks, James!

Contributors

Peter Thomson, Professor Emeritus of Drama at Exeter University, is the author of a score of books on Shakespeare, Brecht and theatre, including *Shakespeare's Theatre, Shakespeare's Professional Career, Brecht's Mother Courage and Her Children* and *English Drama: 1660–1900*. For Intellect he has edited the quarterly journal *Studies in Theatre and Performance*.

Martin Harvey, former Associate Director of the Northcott Theatre, Exeter, has had a varied and acclaimed theatre career as actor, director and writer, with such notable productions as *King Lear, Of Mice and Men* and the one-act opera *Isabella and the Pot of Basil*. He is currently Teaching Fellow in Drama at the University of Exeter.

Thomas Fahy, Director of American Studies at Long Island University, New York, is the author and editor of several notable books, including *Freak Shows and the Modern American Imagination, Considering Alan Ball, Considering Aaron Sorkin* and *Considering David Chase*. He has also published numerous critical articles and two novels, *Night Visions* and *The Unspoken*.

Su Elliott was born in Newcastle upon Tyne and trained at the Guildhall School of Music and Drama in preparation for an acting career that has embraced every part of the industry. Her West End performances include *Can't Pay, Won't Pay* and *Adrian Mole*; for Mike Leigh she appeared in *Secrets and Lies* and, a featured role, *Home Sweet Home*. Her extensive television work includes *Auf Wiedersehen, Pet, Coronation Street* and *Holby City*. Su wrote and performed in a one-woman adaptation of fairy tales to the delight of Fortnam and Mason customers young and old throughout the holiday period, 2007.